CHANGI
UNCHAN

SOCIOLOGY *and* SOCIAL CHANGE

Series Editor: *Alan* **Warde, University of Manchester**

Contents

Series editor's preface

In response to perceived major transformations, social theorists have offered forceful, appealing, but contrasting accounts of the predicament of contemporary western societies and the implications for social life and personal well-being. The speculative and general theses proposed by social theorists must be subjected to evaluation in the light of the best available evidence if they are to serve as guides to understanding and modifying social arrangements. One purpose of sociology, among other social sciences, is to marshal the information necessary to estimate the extent and direction of social change. This series is designed to make such information, and debates about social change, accessible.

The focus of the series is the critical appraisal of general, substantive theories through examination of their applicability to different institutional areas of contemporary societies. Each book introduces key current debates and surveys of existing sociological argument and research about institutional complexes in advanced societies. The integrating theme of the series is the evaluation of the extent of social change. Each author offers explicit and extended evaluation of the pace and direction of social change in a chosen area.

Sara Delamont examines changing gender relations. Her book sticks steadfastly to its primary objective, to try to judge whether, over the last century, women's attitudes, circumstances and behaviours have changed more than those of men. This provides a structure which nicely allows for detailed exposition of studies about gender differences and for a cumulative argument about the significance of changing social institutions. The book explores topics of great contemporary relevance. It expresses strong opinions, some of which are contentious and which will no doubt be considered controversial. This book will be useful not only as a student text but also, because of its strong and distinctive position, as a stimulus to reflection and debate.

Alan Warde

Preface *and* acknowledgements

In 1893, George Gissing published *The Odd Women*, a novel about the roles of women and men as Britain faced the end of the nineteenth century. As Margaret Walters (1980: 4) points out, 'a surprising number of issues raised in *The Odd Women* – the relationship between working-class and middle-class feminism, the difficulty of living out theory, the way sexual feeling may undermine deeply held convictions – are as urgent today'. The novel has been chosen as the *leitmotif* of this book because, in it, 'the men are fearful and old-fashioned; hope lies in the women, who are prepared to confront anarchy and change' (ibid.).

The quotes at the heads of the chapters all come from *The Odd Women*. In the analysis of some topics, the question 'Have women changed while men have not?' is addressed against the century that has elapsed since Gissing wrote that novel. Topics such as life expectancy and the birth rate need to be seen over a long period. However, most of the topics analysed are considered over a 50-year time-scale; that is, since the end of the Second World War in 1945. That is the period for which we have empirical sociological research on Britain, and it is long enough for changes in social structure and the experience of everyday life to manifest themselves.

Good, solid empirical sociology is at the heart of the book, but the text is enlivened with two non-sociological types of material: letters to the problem pages of popular magazines and fictional episodes. Neither of these types of text should be seen as 'the same' as the social science data. Popular magazines carry readers' problems to make an attractive 'read' for their audience, and the problems cannot be seen as 'true' in the same ways social science data are 'true'. However, there is a long history (since the 1920s at least) of their use by social scientists. We must treat them as social products, carefully chosen by the magazines to interest their readers, but they do also dramatize topics that may not surface in orthodox research.

Many of the chapters contain short fictional episodes: one of the freedoms of scholarly work in the social sciences is the tolerance for new forms of text (Wolf 1992; Coffey and Atkinson 1996). Where I have used fictional characters, they are closely based on the findings of sociology: researchers have reported such events, opinions and situations from their investigations.

I have 'fictionalized' them here to make the book more fun to read, to encourage the reader to identify with the core issues and to demonstrate how apparently abstract ideas (such as 'identity' or 'culture') are experienced in everyday life by non-sociologists. To carry through these three aims, I have invented a set of people living in and around a university in a city in the north-east of England, big enough and multicultural enough to embody the sociological themes of the book. To demonstrate the continuing relevance of the questions about sex, gender, sexuality and class raised by Gissing in *The Odd Women*, I have set the fictional episodes in the city and university of Kingsport. Kingsport is the setting for a novel published in 1936 – Winifred Holtby's *South Riding* – which deals with the same themes as Gissing, but about 40 years later in the depression of the inter-war (1929–39) period.

The worlds of Gissing and Holtby span the past, against which the central question of the book, '*Have* women changed while men have stayed the same?', has to be judged.

The structure of the book

There are two introductory chapters, the first of which sets out the central question, 'How do we know if women have changed and men have not?' The second explores the theoretical context of the book. Readers who dislike 'theory' can read it last of all, or skip it altogether, without losing the thread of the rest of the book. From Chapter 3 onwards, the structure of this book is biographical, the same basic organizational principle used for *The Sociology of Women* (Delamont 1980). There are three chapters on growing up in the UK, from childhood to adolescence and into young adulthood (where the impact of class on gender is sharpest), before addressing the central topics in adulthood. The adulthood section of the volume contains four empirical chapters and the conclusions. The four empirical chapters deal with 'Stigma, deviance, bodies and identity', 'Consumption, locality and identity', 'Work and identity' and 'Homelife and identity'.

The feminist perspective of the book

For the purposes of this book, I use a feminist perspective that draws mainly on liberal and radical feminism rather than Marxist or socialist feminism (for good definitions of those schools of feminism, see Humm 1992). I focus on imbalances between males and females in Britain (a classic liberal feminist tactic) and critique the knowledge base of research on gender (a classic radical feminist tactic). I share a definition of feminism with Donna Haraway (1989: 290): 'Feminist theory and practice . . . seek to explain and change historical systems of sexual difference, whereby "men" and "women" are socially constituted and positioned in relations of hierarchy and antagonism'.

Acknowledgements

I am grateful to Lesley Edwards for starting the word-processing of this book and to Karen Chivers, Jackie Swift and Rosemary Jones for completing it. Paul Atkinson has been remarkably patient as I insisted on rehearsing the ideas presented here even when he had work of his own to complete. His trenchant criticism and constant support continue to sustain me.

Part **one**
INTRODUCTORY ISSUES

Part one contains two introductory chapters. The first sets out the central question, 'Have women changed while men have not?' The second introduces key theoretical issues about contemporary sociological approaches to the study of gender.

1 Introduction

With a fluttering heart Virginia made what haste she could homewards.
The interview had filled her with a turmoil of strange new thoughts. It
was the first time in her life that she had spoken with a woman daring
enough to think and act for herself.

(Gissing 1893/1980: 24)

Virginia is a central character in *The Odd Women*. She is living through the
changes in sex roles that convulsed Britain in the 1880s and 1890s. In the
extract she is confused because she has met a pair of feminists, the heroines
of the novel, who are training women to earn their own living and exist
without male breadwinners. The heady mix of economic independence and
revolutionary ideas about sex roles is the central focus of the novel. Contemporary thinking on women's economic roles, ideas about sex roles and 'fluttering hearts' is the subject of this book.

What was life like for males and females in the 1890s, in the early 1950s,
and has it changed in the new century? Are females today *more* changed from
their great-grandmothers and their great-great-great-grandmothers than males
are from their great-grandfathers and their great-great-great-grandfathers?
This is the question that is revisited in each chapter of the book.

This introductory chapter deals with three topics:

1 The received wisdom that women have changed and men have not.
2 The place of men and women in modernity and the impact of
postmodernity.
3 The structure of the book.

It sets up the central intellectual issue addressed, explains the concepts of
gender, modernity and postmodernity, and outlines the purpose and structure of the book. The central issue explored throughout the book is, 'Have
women changed while men have failed to change?'

The central issue

A consistent *motif* in much of the social science of the past 15 years is that
women's expectations and behaviours have changed while those of men have

not. Researchers have reported that female respondents to surveys and inter-view questions have expressed views that are strikingly unlike those of girls and women in earlier generations, and that their behaviour is also different from that of their mothers, grandmothers and great-grandmothers. These researchers have argued that the girls and women they have studied have adapted to changing economic conditions, such as the decline of traditional heavy industries like mining and steelmaking, and to ideas such as individual-ism and self-determination better than the boys and men they live and work with. They claim that women were responding to, and coping with, the social changes in their neighbourhoods and regions 'better' than men were.

Such claims were advanced in, for example, *Working Class without Work* (Weis 1989), *Making the Difference* (Connell *et al*. 1982), the Women Risk and Aids Project (WRAP) and the Men Risk and Aids Project (MRAP)(Holland *et al*. 1991, 1993). Weis studied adolescents in an American city where the steelworks had closed, destroying the main source of male employment after a century of prosperity. She argued that the adolescent girls had recognized the end of the old order and were planning for a post-industrial way of life, while the adolescent boys had not. They still wanted traditional manual jobs for themselves with wives who did not work outside the home and showed deference to the male wage earner.

Connell and his team reported similar divergences among Australian adolescents, especially in working-class families, where the disappearance of traditional male manual work was poorly understood by parents or adolescent boys. Working-class girls and the middle classes were abandoning the ideal of a traditional division of labour in favour of more flexible working and domestic arrangements. In the UK, Holland and her collaborators reported young women struggling to escape from the sexual double standard in the face of young men enforcing and reinforcing it.

These three projects, all focusing on young men and women, together with others discussed later in this book, meant that by the late 1980s there was some consensus that a gap was growing between the sexes regarding expectations about adult sex roles in employment and at home. Young men were, just like their counterparts in the 1880s, fearful of the future, whereas women looked forward to greater change. Secondary sources, such as my own *Sex Roles and the School* (Delamont 1990), began to generalize on the basis of such studies. Once proposed by social scientists using research on young, child-free women, the idea of women changing and men remaining the same quickly spread far beyond its evidential base and became a generaliza-tion, a cliché and a myth. The myth was then promulgated in popular books (Harman 1993; Coward 1999) and spread into journalism.

Once the idea of one sex changing while the other did not was around, a backlash began. Some social scientists and some popular commentators argued that the evidential base was not there: that the social scientists had *not* shown that women had changed. The work of Catherine Hakim (1995, 1996) is a typical example of such an argument. Other writers, especially the exponents of the 'new' evolutionary psychology, claimed that men cannot change because of their biological and evolutionary drives to compete, fight and have sex with as many partners as possible to spread their genes at the expense of those of other men (Ridley 1993). These writers argue either that women have not and cannot change because of their biology, or that women must not be allowed to change because the social damage caused by the unnecessary, displaced men will destroy the social system (Dench 1994, 1996; Fukuyama 1999). These latter groups of commentators blame feminism for *either* making false claims that women have changed when the vast majority have not, *or* for encouraging women to change and abandon old-fashioned men. Leading biologists reject evolutionary psychology (see Rose 1998; Rose and Rose 2000) and it does not feature in the argument of this book.

So, while the 1980s saw a number of studies in several different formerly industrialized, capitalist countries, suggesting that as traditional heavy industry declined the sexes responded in different ways to that de-industrialization, in the 1990s a debate took place in the quality newspapers and on radio and television about sex roles that moved far beyond any evidence available. The need for carefully conducted research was acute. However, three factors impeded the progress of carefully conducted research in general and that on sex roles in particular. First, in Britain and America, government funds for social research were reduced by right-wing regimes and there was political inference with the research agenda. (The most famous example in Britain was Mrs Thatcher vetoing a survey on sexual behaviour that was needed to inform health education to prevent the spread of HIV/AIDS.) Second, the very processes of de-industrialization were breaking down the basic categories formerly used by researchers. For example, as co-habitation becomes more and more common, the simple distinctions between 'single, married, divorced, widowed' are simply unusable in research. Third, trends in sociology were moving away from careful empirical research on social structures and institutions towards studies of the media and cultural studies, fuelled by a theoretical shift to 'postmodernism'.

The popular media attention to the claim that women had changed and men had not was relevant to feminist social scientists because it drew on their research and it encouraged debate about the feminist 'political' agenda. For example, how does a society prevent rape or reduce the percentage of old women living in poverty? However, the same mass media in the past 20 years has also claimed that 'feminism is dead' and that the new evolutionary psychology proves that sex differences are biological and so men 'cannot' do the ironing or change a baby's nappies. At exactly the point where feminist social scientists needed both to defend their research base and marshall their arguments about the 'problem of men', their own theoretical position was assailed by a new intellectual fashion, postmodernism, which threatened the very existence of a feminist social science. The purpose of this book is to explore the contested terrain on which these disputes are taking place. This chapter explores the proposition that women have changed and men have not and the two main criticisms of that proposition. The impact of postmodernism on feminist sociology is explored in Chapter 2.

Harriet Harman has been a Labour MP since 1983, and was briefly a minister in the 1997–2001 Blair administration. In 1993, while in Opposition, she published a popular book called *The Century Gap*, subtitled '20th Century Man. 21st Century Woman: How both Sexes can Bridge the Century Gap'.

Harman argued that 'women have left the twentieth century behind' and 'Twenty-first century women have arrived, a century ahead of time' (p. 1). In contrast, men were still 'a century behind' (p. 3) – that is, trying to live in the same ways as their ancestors of the industrial era in the post-industrial world. Harman is a politician, not a sociologist. Her hypothesis needs to be tested using the research evidence. At the same time, Harman's hypothesis also has to be tested against the claims of the 'biological' determinists (Rose and Rose 2000). This would be hard to do even in an era when there was consensus about what good 'malestream' research looked like and what good feminist research looked like. However, in the twenty-first century, there is no longer any consensus about what good research looks like. There is, therefore, no consensus about what counts as research evidence to test Harman's hypothesis, or to challenge the position of Fukuyama (1999) and Dench (1996), which is similar to Harman's about women but demands that women must change back to where men are, or indeed about whether there can be any future for feminist research at all.

The year 2000 is a hard time to write a feminist critique of the literature on women and men because feminism is under attack, both as a political movement and as a variety of theory in social science. Apart from the routine hostility and abuse that feminism has always attracted because it challenges the male-dominated, patriarchal *status quo*, there are serious claims that feminism is dead. Many pundits say feminism is dead because modern Britain has gender equality. Others argue feminism is outmoded because young women are not interested in feminism, seeing it as a sad ideology espoused by their mothers, lesbians and ugly women in dungarees who cannot attract men (Skeggs 1997; Pilcher 1998).

Scholars who believe feminist social science is dead argue on more academic grounds. The most successful and high-profile of these scholars argue that feminist social science is dead because of postmodernism. Among scholars who argue for feminist analyses believing they are not outmoded (e.g. Oakley 1998, 2000), there are many disputes about what topics to study, what methods to use, how to analyse the data and which theoretical schools within feminism (Humm 1992) to acclaim. This book does not attempt to adjudicate between these feuding sisterhoods. It is important to recognize that there are differences between the types of research that feminists do and the uses to which they may be put (Roseneil 1995). There are also arguments as to whether 30 years of feminist sociology have actually made any difference to the mainstream of the discipline (Delamont, forthcoming). These are important, but this book focuses on a practical question about the everyday lives of women and men.

The 'women have changed, men have not' claim

The scholars who first proposed that women had changed their ideas about how men and women should organize work and the division of labour in the home because of the disappearance of the old heavy industries, while men had not, mainly drew on data gathered from young people. Weis (1989) conducted a study of adolescents in Rochester, a city in North America, where the steel-based industries had collapsed and the highly paid, safe jobs for men bashing metal had vanished. She found that the young women had 'written-off' Rochester and traditional marriage, in which a man is the bread-winner, and planned to go to college, get qualifications for new jobs and follow employment to other cities. The young men, in contrast, yearned for the good old days to return, in which they could work in the steel industry and support full-time housewives who would greet them with home-made food when they came off their shifts. In Australia, Connell and his co-workers (1982) argued something similar, reporting that these tensions were more acute in some ethnic groups than others, and more problematic for working-class Australians than for the professional classes. Around the same time, a study of British couples who had just got married (Mansfield and Collard 1988) found that, when their behaviour was investigated, their division of labour was very traditional. Women cooked, men did the DIY and both sexes felt this was 'natural'. However, the women wanted a different kind of emotional relationship from the marriage than the men and were unhappy because it had not materialized (this study is dealt with in more detail in Chapter 9).

A few studies of people under 30 in the 1980s are not sufficient to make claims about all ages, classes and countries. However, statistical evidence, such as the increased proportion of women petitioning for divorce, allowed Harman (1993) to set out her thesis in *The Century Gap*, outlined earlier in the chapter. Harman believes women have already entered the twenty-first century, in which both sexes are in parent-friendly paid employment and both take equal parts in the physical and emotional work of raising children and running a home. For this to be achieved, Harman argues, men have to change:

> clearly things cannot go on as they are. It is neither possible nor desirable to turn the clock back. The emancipation of women cannot be reversed; and even if it was [*sic*], the result would be total economic collapse.
>
> (Harman 1993: 8)

Harman's is a popular book, like Dench's (1994, 1996) twice published volume. Dench argues that it is desirable, possible and even essential for social order that Britain returns to the traditional division of labour in the home and the workplace. Both have in common a belief that there is a century gap. In the rest of this book, that belief will be tested, using evidence, especially recent sociology and official statistics as published in *Social Trends* (1989, 1999). Throughout the book, differences other than sex are also stressed. Class, region and ethnicity are important divisions in the UK, and many generalizations about 'women' or 'men' have to be qualified. Women with degrees in Essex are not living in 'the same' Britain as unskilled catholic women in Northern Ireland, unskilled Sikh women in Cardiff or unskilled Muslim women in Bradford. These differences are as important as any between that graduate in Essex and a male graduate in Wrexham, Inverness or Carlisle. Class divisions are deep and wide in Britain, and differences based on region, religion and ethnicity also matter.

There has been such an explosion of research on men and women in the past 20 years that a small book could easily be swamped. Every sentence could have a dozen references and lead to half a dozen tables. To make this book readable, I have illustrated the main points with exemplary studies and left out many other good, interesting, relevant and thought-provoking invest-igations. Each chapter gives particular prominence to a project, which, for me, captures the central issue of that chapter: studies which I would have been proud to have done myself, which are landmarks. The 'further reading' at the end of each chapter provides a reference on each topic which has an excellent bibliography. Please use that reference to go into the literature that interests you. With these points in mind, let me end this chapter with a comment on gender equality from Beck (1994: 27), which addresses both our central themes: 'A society in which men and women were really equal . . . would without doubt be a new modernity'.

Verdict

The claim that women have changed while men have not is worth invest-igating, although the intellectual climate is not an ideal one for testing such a claim.

Further reading

Dench, G. (1996) *Transforming Men*. New Brunswick, NJ: Transaction Books.
Harman, H. (1993) *The Century Gap*. London: Vermilion.
Pilcher, J. (1999) *Women in Contemporary Britain*. London: Routledge.
The first two books set out the claim. The third is a serious work of sociology, offering an alternative view from mine.

2 Theoretical dilemmas

I don't care what results, if only women are made strong and self-reliant and nobly independent.

(Gissing 1893/1980: 136)

Here Mary Barfoot, one of the two heroines of *The Odd Women*, sets out her vision for feminism. A century later, there are women who are strong, self-reliant and nobly independent. This is largely a result of the feminist movement, which opened up education and employment to women. There are many different histories of British feminism (e.g. Banks 1981) and its consequences. The position of women today, and the state of the sociological ideas about them, can be attributed to the achievements of each of the three 'waves' of feminism.

For the purposes of this book, feminism is divided into three broad phases. First-wave feminism, from about 1848 to 1918, focused on getting women rights in public spheres, especially the vote, education and entry to middle-class jobs such as medicine. The views of these feminists, at least as they expressed them in public, were puritan about sex, alcohol, dress and behaviour. The second wave, from 1918 to 1968, was concerned with social reform (such as free school meals for poor children and health care for poor women) and 'revolution' in the private sphere: the right to contraception, the end of the sexual double standard, and so on. Third-wave feminism, from 1968 to the present, has been concerned with public issues again (equal pay, an end to sex discrimination in employment, pensions, mortgages, etc.) and with making formerly private issues (such as rape and domestic violence) matters of public concern and reform. The third wave has also produced a revolution in the scholarly knowledge bases of most disciplines, such as feminist sociology, which is of concern to women in education if to no-one else. In this third wave, all the humanities and social sciences have developed feminist sub-specialisms: there are feminist geographies, histories, political science, psychology, and so on. In this chapter, some of the central ideas of feminist sociology are outlined, together with the main disputes within feminist sociology surrounding postmodernism, addressing the dilemmas explored by Roseneil (1995).

That all sounds very dull. To make the issues more vivid and immediate, I introduce here the first of the fictional episodes. Let us move to Kingsport and see how the issues are a problem for students.

Kingsport University 2005: Scene 2.1

It is nearly the end of the autumn semester at Kingsport University, on the coast of the South Riding of Yorkshire. One bleak late November evening, four students are gathered in the communal kitchen of a flat in Carne Hall, wrestling with their essays for module SOC101: Introductory Sociology, due in on 1 December. Lovel Brown, an African Caribbean man from Leeds, reads out: 'What are the most significant debates that have characterized sociology over the past two decades? Show how *one* debate developed in the UK'. He and his companions, Emma Tuke, Chloe Beddows and Barnabas Holly, fall to debating whether the best debate to choose for their essays from those outlined in their lecture course is the crisis of Marxism, the collapse of positivism, the fragmentation of feminist sociology or the rise of postmodernism. All four confess that they are hopelessly confused about postmodernism, post-industrial society and reflexive modernity, having 'got lost' in Dr Prizethorpe's lecture.

Any student has a right to feel confused about postmodernism as a theory and its relationships to post-industrialism. The mythical Dr Prizethorpe can be excused for giving a confusing lecture, because three intellectual crises have 'hit' social science at once and, if we are interested in gender, a fourth debate is also confusing the issue. In this chapter, they are separated, briefly explained and the position taken for this book is outlined.

In 1968–71, social science was disrupted by a series of political events with global reverberations: the Soviet invasion of Czechoslovakia, the cultural revolution in China and the upheavals in the capitalist industrial societies where manual workers were engaged in industrial unrest, students in political revolt, the gay and women's liberation movements burst into public consciousness, and many ethnic groups in the USA, especially African Americans, Latino-Americans and Native-Americans, erupted into political activity including violence (for an analysis, see Gouldner 1970; Giddens 1981). The complacent, consensual social science had failed to predict any of those eruptions, and the dominant school of thought was unable to explain them after the event. The twenty-first century finds social science in a state of uncertainty and disputation, which is much healthier than the complacent orthodoxies of the mid-1960s, but more confusing for students such as Lovel, Ben, Chloe and Emma. Two of the three general sociology journals in Britain, *The British Journal of Sociology* (Vol. 51, No. 1) and *Sociology* (Vol. 35, No. 1), produced special millennial issues in 2000. A brief glance at these contrasting volumes reveals how diverse the discipline is.

The collapse of communism, or at least of the Soviet empire and, therefore, of state socialism in Europe and much of Asia, symbolized by the fall of the Berlin Wall in 1989 (Borneman 1992), has led to a crisis in Marxist social science. At the same time, the rise of a theoretical position called 'postmodernism' (explained below) has convulsed most social sciences. Meanwhile, the twin economic pressures of the globalization of production (where most manufacturing is being moved to the Third World/underdeveloped countries where labour is exploited, expendable and therefore cheap) and the de-industrialization of the capitalist 'industrialized' economies have changed, and are changing rapidly, the working lives of ordinary men and women. Simultaneously, there has been globalization of communication: with satellite and telecommunications allowing both more democratic sharing of information *and* greater control of it by the owners of the transmitters (Albrow 1996). Overlying all these seismic shifts was an artificial 'hysteria': millennial fervour. As the year 2000 approached for the *Christian* world (Gould 1998), we were still in a state of expectancy: we were in the *fin-de-siècle* (Pahl 1996; Showalter 1996). At the ends of the eighteenth and nineteenth centuries, the western world experienced political and intellectual ferments, so it was not surprising to find equivalent disarray in 1998–99. This sense of unease, especially disquiet about sex roles and sexuality, common at the ends of centuries, persisted – although the Christian 2000 is not 2000 for Islam, Jews or the Japanese, who have different calendars – even though we all knew *rationally* that this was a date we had set for ourselves, that it is arbitrary, that it changed nothing.

There are four shorthand labels for the current era, espoused by different sociologists: post-industrial, the postmodern, post-traditional reflexive modernity (Beck *et al.* 1994) or, as Beck (1992) calls it, the 'risk society'. Beck (1994: 24) has argued that conventional sociology, or as he prefers to call it 'the ageing sociology of modernization', has to be replaced, because the economic base of modernity has gone and so too must the sociology of modernity. Scholars interested in the lives of women in Britain such as Bradley (1996) and Walby (1997) have also drawn attention to these changes in the economic base of British society, and to the implications of de-industrialization and globalization for women. For women who used feminist sociology to explain the role of women in a modern society, calls such as Beck's to replace the 'ageing sociology of modernization' with a new sociology of post-traditional reflexive modernity have been particularly problematic. This is because the new postmodern sociology does not 'fit' alongside or on top of any of the popular varieties of feminist sociology, but rather undermines them. For feminists, one type of replacement sociology, creating a postmodern sociology to explain the postmodern world, is particularly problematic because it challenges feminism itself. Accordingly, postmodernism is the focus of the next section.

Postmodernism

Lyon (1999) presents a clear and well-written introduction to postmodern theorizing. This section defines postmodernism, shows what a restricted sector of British society is interested in it, explains why feminists have to be in that restricted sector, and what the implications for the rest of the volume are. In the next section, after a brief explanation of postmodern theory, I focus on how the theory is problematic for feminists, for feminist sociology and for empirical investigation of women's role in contemporary Britain.

Postmodernism is an intellectual challenge to feminist sociologists and anti-sexist campaigners. It is a typical *fin-de-siècle* ideological movement and it is tempting to treat it as similar to panics about alien abductions now or anarchist plots a century ago. However, we need to learn from history; as Vicinus (1985) showed, it was a *fin-de-siècle* ideological movement (Freudianism) that destroyed the intellectual underpinning of first-wave feminism, so we cannot write off postmodernism as merely an end of century malaise.

Postmodernism argues that we have reached the end of the Enlightenment Project: the faith that we can find a neutral standpoint from which to gather objective facts and scientific truth about the world. Postmodernists claim that, in 2001, it is no longer possible for a thinking person to believe in objectivity, truth or 'science', because the epistemological basis for a belief in objectivity has been destroyed. For 200 years, elite white men in Western Europe and North America believed that objective research was possible in science, social science and the humanities. Today, a subset of such men (the postmodernists) are arguing that this belief was misguided: objectivity was actually the biased perspective of those same elite white men who were lulling themselves into a false sense of security by claiming objectivity. What they thought was objectivity was actually just *their* view of the world (and the views of women, the working class, the other religions of the world, the citizens of Japan, China, Russia and the whole of the Third World were deemed 'non-scientific' and ignored).

The postmodernist subset of white men are having their biggest impact in arts and social sciences. So, postmodernism argues:

> The essence of the post-modern argument is that the dualisms which continue to dominate Western thought are inadequate for understanding a world of multiple causes and effects interacting in complex and non-linear ways, all of which are rooted in a limitless array of historical and cultural specificities.
>
> (Lather 1991: 21)

This is a complicated way of saying that a scientific method invented 400 years ago, when the world was divided into self-contained chunks that did not interact, is inadequate for the planet in 2005. An amusing exemplification of what postmodernism 'means' was printed in the correspondence page of the *Times Literary Supplement*. There had been an angry debate about the beneficial or malevolent influence postmodernism was having in various intellectual areas, with some letters printed asking plaintively what the term meant. The following letter effectively closed the correspondence. It is about baseball, but a similar story would fit cricket or tennis.

> Sir, – Paul Boghossian mentions Stanley Fish's article, in which Fish refers to the meaning of "ball" and "strike". I have not read Fish and so do not know if he mentions a well-known piece of baseball philosophy.

Three umpires are discussing how they do their job. The first, who is also the least experienced, says, "I call 'em as they are". The second, who has been in the game a little longer, says, "I call 'em as I see 'em". The third and most experienced says, "They're nothing till I call 'em". These three could be characterised as objectivism, relativism and post-modernism respectively.

(Andrew Rawlinson, *Times Literary Supplement*, 3 January 1997, p. 17)

The third umpire was pointing out that there is nothing objective about whether a pitch is legal or not, only a human decision and label. A legal pitch is a ball so labelled by the umpire.

Sociology has schools of though which are based on each of the three 'isms' named by Andrew Rawlinson. Sociologists who believe that it is possible to gather data 'scientifically' and that those data are facts are objectivists (often called positivists in sociology). Those who adopt the idea that different social groups have different understandings of the world and that the world is socially constructed are relativists (or constructionists or interactionists). Postmodernists place stress on *discourse*: on how humans create realities by their speech about it. For them, there is no objectivity, only human discourse.

Disputes between positivists, interactionists and postmodernists matter in social science, which is why Lovel, Chloe, Emma and Barnabas have to wrestle with the ideas. The science students in the next flat doing a set of physics problems (Tobias 1990; Downey and Lucena 1997) would not be expected to have heard of the term, any more than members of the Kingsport professional soccer, rugby union and rugby league teams would be. They can play football without worrying about postmodernism, just as in their everyday work scientists are untroubled by such concerns (Gilbert and Mulkay 1984). Readers of this book share with Lovel and his friends the need to understand postmodernism and the other upheavals (globalization, post-industrialization, etc.) I have outlined. Most people in the UK have no need to grapple with such unsettling ideas. Even among the highly educated minority in Britain, only those working in humanities and social sciences need to understand postmodernism. People working in the professions (medicine, law, accountancy, architecture, etc.) and those in science and engineering do not have to bother. This is a major cleavage among the highly educated in contemporary Britain, between scientists and the postmodernists in humanities and social sciences today. The dispute has been nicknamed the 'Science Wars' and was inflamed by the Sokal hoax (Mackenzie 1999), when a scientist wrote a load of nonsense in a pastiche of post-modern style and got it published. Lovel, Emma, Chloe and Barnabas need to understand the debate; the majority of students do not.

The rise of postmodernist ideas is only a 'problem' for an intellectual elite, because the dominant set of propositions it is challenging was only ever the platform of the intellectual elite. The Enlightenment Project was never a mass phenomenon, it was always an elite concern. The masses were never part of the Enlightenment Project because the elite never wanted, or never managed, to educate the masses sufficiently to make them accept rationality, objectivity or the scientific method. We can remind ourselves that only those classes or fragments of classes which had access to elaborated code speech (Bernstein 1971) could buy into the Enlightenment Project, and that the Enlightenment Project has been, for 200 years, the habitus of the intelligentsia (Bourdieu 1996).

Most people in Britain were never given the chance to learn enough about science to grasp its basic premises, the dream of the Enlightenment Project. The current row over trialling genetically modified foods, the widespread 'belief' in astrology, the persistence of smoking and the folk beliefs about HIV/AIDS, all show that most people do not 'live' in the same world as those who are highly educated. The campaigns for public understanding of science are only necessary because the masses have had no intellectual share in the Englightenment Project.

The Enlightenment Project was also limited by geographical and religious factors. It was originally a Protestant phenomenon that subsequently spread to intellectual Roman Catholics. In large areas of the world, there was no Enlightenment. This point was made forcibly in a letter to the *London Review of Books*, in which K.W.C. Sinclair-Loutit recounted a conversation with a proud Orthodox Serb in 1994:

> My friend, a good Serbian Orthodox Christian, was of a culture continuous with that of the Byzantine Empire. The Renaissance, the Reformation, the Enlightenment and the Industrial Revolution had not touched him.
>
> (*London Review of Books*, 16 April 1998, p. 4)

Postmodernism is not a problem if the Enlightenment never occurred in your culture.

For Lovel, Chloe, Barnabas and Emma, who have chosen to study sociology, these are important debates. In the short term, they have to choose an essay title and address it; in the longer term, they have 3 years to get to grips with globalization, reflexive modernity and even postmodernism. For students interested in feminism, the conflict between feminism and postmodernism has to be confronted immediately.

Feminism and postmodernism

Imagine another part of Kingsport University:

Kingsport University 2005: Scene 2.2

It is a late November evening. In the coffee shop in the Sarah Burton Building, three women's studies students are planning their seminar presentation for the whole class. Jean Marsh is a primary teacher, Lisa Warbuckle a social worker and Penny Stathers works in local government. They are all graduates in their late thirties and are supposed to be staging a debate on postmodernism and feminist theory. Jean has read work by Jane Flax and is convinced that feminist postmodernism is the way forward. Lisa has read Somer

Brodribb and has decided that postmodernism is 'about as much use to feminism as slug pellets are to slugs!' Penny is sceptical about all theory: she wants to focus on practical issues and is wondering whether she has chosen the wrong course. Grace Pinker – an engineering undergraduate – overhears a bit of the conversation and wonders what planet they are from.

Postmodernist ideas have been particularly controversial within feminist circles and while Penny's position seems attractive, it is not possible for feminist sociologists to ignore theoretical/intellectual currents.

The universities in the UK are full of people enthusiastic about post-modernism, so feminists have to respond to it. Feminists have been divided in their responses to postmodernism (Oakley 1998). Some have been deeply suspicious of the founding fathers of postmodernism, who are overwhelmingly middle-class, white men in secure jobs in industrialized countries. Thus Fox-Genovese (1986: 134) has commented:

> Surely it is no coincidence that the Western white male elite proclaimed the death of the subject at precisely the moment at which it might have had to share that status with the women and people of other races and classes who were beginning to challenge its supremacy.

Fox-Genovese is an African American woman. She and other women, such as Hoff (1994) and Brodribb (1992), have stressed that the origins of postmodernism lie in Paris after 1945, with white men (Levi-Strauss, Lacan, Foucault, Derrida, Lyotard) who were all sexist and misogynist. Foucault, in particular, was a gay man with a marked dislike for women, whose work can be read as more misogynist than the other founders. Feminists opposed to postmodernism regard it as a social theory developed by men specifically intended to retain men's intellectual dominance. These women see postmodernism as a social theory explicitly designed to mystify and exclude women from intellectual debate and, therefore, top jobs in elite universities. This is what Somer Brodribb (1992: 7–8) means when she states 'post-modernism is the cultural capital of late patriarchy'. Brodribb is a forceful opponent of postmodern ideas, arguing that feminist social science must be built on intellectual ideas originated by women. Fox-Genovese, Hoff and Brodribb do not want to stick with positivist sociology, hanging on to the Englightenment Project, but they do not want to join the postmodern band-wagon either.

There are distinguished feminist social scientists who ignore the misogynist male origins of postmodernism because they see it as liberating for women. One such enthusiast, Patti Lather (1991), has already been quoted (see p. 12). Similarly, another enthusiast, Jane Flax, argues that 'Post-modern philosophers seek to throw into radical doubt beliefs . . . derived from the Enlightenment (Flax 1990: 41). She lists among the beliefs thrown into doubt: the existence of a stable self, reason, an objective foundation for knowledge, and universalism. She forcefully expresses this:

> The meanings – or even existence – of concepts essential to all forms of Enlightenment metanarrative (reason, history, science, self, knowledge,

power, gender, and the inherent superiority of Western culture) have been subjected to increasingly corrosive attacks.

(Flax 1993: 450)

For Lather and Flax, feminism had already challenged the male Enlightenment concepts of 'reason', 'the stable self', 'universalism', 'history', 'science', 'power', 'gender', 'knowledge', 'objectivity' and the 'inherent superiority of western culture'. Challenging all these ideas was central to the intellectual agenda of contemporary feminism. None of these ideas has been acceptable to feminists since 1968: all have been attacked. The feminist slogan 'the personal is political', for example, challenges the Enlightenment ideas of objectivity, reason, universalism and the stable self. From this starting point, Jane Flax (1993: 447) argues that much feminist scholarship has been 'critical of the contents' of the Enlightenment dream, yet simultaneously 'unable to abandon them'. For Flax this is not a proper feminist response. Because the Enlightenment was a *male* cosmology, feminists must abandon it to create their own. Flax is confident that the insights of postmodernism will set women free from a childlike state in which we wait for 'higher authorities' to rescue us, clinging to a naive myth of 'sisterhood'.

For every Flax welcoming postmodernism (e.g. Flax 1990), there are other women who are anxious that it will destroy feminism or who are mounting a vigorous attack upon it (e.g. Brodribb 1992; Oakley 1998). The debate is highly polemicized and Brodribb, in particular, reaches rhetorical heights which leave most of us gasping. Her opponents – those feminists who wish to become postmodernists or adapt postmodernism to their own ends – are called 'ragpickers in the bins of male ideas' (Flax 1993: xxiii). The violence of the debate, and hence the anxieties underlying it, can be seen in a highly charged argument in *Women's History Review* between Hoff (1994, 1996), Kent (1996) and Ramazanoglu (1996).

Having set out the main positions in the debate over feminism and postmodernism, the next section explains my position and the stance of the book.

Feminism, postmodernism and this book

I am personally ambivalent about postmodernism and its role in sociology, especially in sociological thinking by and about women. This is partly because the women who built schools, universities, hospitals and careers for women, and got us the vote, were overwhelmed by a parallel intellectual fashion in the first two decades of the twentieth century. First-wave feminism was intellectually destroyed by Freudianism (for the bases of this claim, see Delamont 1992a). If today's feminism is to survive postmodernism, those of us who are feminists have to be particularly careful to scrutinize it, and then ensure we are riding it like a surfer rather than being drowned by it (Coffey and Delamont 2000; Delamont 2000b). There is no point in writing a book about women and men in contemporary Britain which ignores the debates over postmodernism. That would be as silly as assuming that 50 per cent of British workers were in agriculture (the figure in 1851) instead of two per cent (the figure in 1981).

However, my problem with such commentators as Dench (1996) and Fukuyama (1999), who claim that feminists and the chattering classes are destroying the family and therefore society by encouraging women to abandon traditional family life, is that they do not ground their commentary in high-quality empirical research. The tensions within sociology and within feminism caused by the rise of postmodernism, and the other changes arising from post-industrialism and globalization, are one theme running through the book. The other central concern is a much more mundane one: facts about whether women have changed their attitudes and behaviour since 1893 or 1951 whereas men have not. In an attempt to balance the theoretical and conceptual debates about post-industrial or risk society and about postmodernism and feminism with some material about real men, women and children living in modern Britain, the book uses research evidence ('facts') in an old-fashioned, or 'modern', as opposed to a post-modern way.

I am acutely aware that this is not an intellectually coherent position. The *text* is influenced by one current associated with postmodernism: the fictional episodes, the use of 'evidence' from the mass media and the presence of the author in the debates are all common in books by authors who espouse postmodernism. Bradley (1996: 3) captures my dilemma when she writes: 'post-modern approaches sit uneasily with study of material factors such as inequality and deprivation and those influenced by the ideas of postmodernism have tended to avoid these topics'. Bradley sets herself to 'pull together' traditional approaches to inequalities with the 'newer perspectives'. I, too, am trying to meld two approaches.

Both first-wave and third-wave feminism have been concerned with political action, with improving the economic status of women, with tackling violence against women, with educating women, with raising the status of women's and children's health, and with ensuring that female voices and experiences are treated as seriously as those of males. One of the major differences between first-wave and third-wave feminisms in the English-speaking world is particularly relevant to sociology: attitudes to knowledge. In general, the first-wave feminists were concerned to open up academic secondary education, higher education and professional training to girls and women. In an era when only males could study algebra, Greek, Hebrew, Latin and the physical sciences, the goal of feminists was to open them to females and prove that women could excel at them. There were a few feminists who queried the epistemological status of the male knowledge base, but this was not a major preoccupation. When women were forbidden to learn male knowledge, it was necessary to gain access to it first (Delamont 1989, 1992a).

By the late 1960s, when third-wave feminism arose, women in Britain and the USA were allowed access to most spheres of male knowledge. The third-wave feminist movement has focused on challenging the epistemological basis, the methods and the content of 'mainstream' or '*male*stream' knowledge. This shows in the academic departments, degree courses and textbooks in women's studies; in the feminist publishing houses and feminist lists in the established houses; in the social science methods textbooks; and in arts and social science disciplines where there are feminist journals, women's caucuses in the learned societies and books on many feminist topics. Sociology has been a fertile ground for feminist challenges to the knowledge base.

To conclude this chapter, I provide an explanation of the varieties of feminist sociology. If we return to Kingsport, we can see why this is necessary.

Back to Kingsport

In the first Kingsport scenario (see p. 10), four undergraduates were discussing which essay to write for their introductory course. If Lovel, Emma, Chloe and Barnabas decided to avoid the postmodernism essay question and write about feminism instead, their task would be relatively straightforward. They 'only' have to sort out the varieties of feminist sociology in the nineteenth and then the twentieth century.

The feminist movement of the nineteenth century certainly had several different strands of thought within it. Olive Banks (1981), writing of the British and American scene, separated three currents of thought. These were the evangelical, the enlightenment and the communitarian socialist traditions, each with its roots in the late eighteenth century. The evangelical feminists who drew their inspiration from their religious beliefs – Quakers, Unitarians and other non-conformists – focused on social issues. Their feminism was closely related to campaigns to abolish slavery, introduce temperance, and attack prostitution, pornography and 'immorality'. The second group of feminists drew inspiration from the Enlightenment, which swept intellectual circles in Europe in the late eighteenth century. John Stuart Mill and Mary Wollstonecraft are the central figures in this tradition. They emphasized the importance of rational thought, evidence, and the theoretical ideas of 'rights', 'autonomy' and individualism. The communitarian socialist tradition grew out of the French Saint-Simonian movement, and then added Marxist ideas in the latter part of the century. Among those who were inspired by socialism are those Banks called Utopians, who wanted communal living, 'free love' and pooled child-rearing. When first-wave feminism died in the early years of the twentieth century, these three intellectual strands all withered.

Second-wave feminism was not primarily an intellectual movement, it was mainly practical. When third-wave feminism arose, it, like first-wave feminism, had intellectual concerns intertwined with its campaigns. In third-wave feminism, commonly dated from the late 1960s, most commentators see three major divisions: liberal feminism, radical or separatist feminism, and Marxist or socialist feminism. In addition, today most scholars would wish to separate black feminism, on the grounds that all the other three failed to incorporate racism and black experience into their analyses (see, for example, Humm 1992; Roman 1992; Weiner 1994). Abbott and Wallace (1990) provide an excellent introduction to feminist perspectives in sociology, whose strengths and weaknesses can only be briefly outlined here.

Liberal feminists are reformists: they believe that if the realities of women's disadvantage are established and publicized, a rational democracy will change to redress the disadvantage. In sociology, liberal feminists want to ensure that gender is taken seriously as a research variable, and that social theory incorporates gender. So a liberal feminist will argue that studies of social mobility should include men and women in the sample, and explore the social mobility of both sexes.

Marxist, or socialist, feminists see women's oppression as a consequence of capitalism, which also oppresses men. Politically their goal is to overthrow capitalism but to include sex equality as a central tenet of the replacement social organization. Within sociology, Marxist and socialist feminists (e.g. Barrett 1988) explore the economic base of women's disadvantages.

Liberal and Marxist feminists frequently share a research strategy, which is to seek facts and evidence – often statistical evidence – about sex inequalities. Radical feminists are more often focused on challenging the categories of sociological debate, such as Stanley and Wise's (1983) rejection of the distinction between 'public' and 'private' spheres. Radical or separatist feminists believe that patriarchy (male domination) is evident in all societies and has been throughout human history. In politics, such feminists seek to build all-female communities grounded in women's values, such as the Greenham Peace Camp. The sociological argument of radical feminism is explored by Walby (1997).

Post-modern feminists and feminists who advocate post-modern sociology can be found among liberal and radical feminists. The debates about postmodernism cut across the four types of feminism, although very few black or Marxist feminists are attracted to postmodernism because of its rejection of essentialisms such as 'race' and 'class'. Lovel and his friends can produce straightforward essays about liberal, Marxist, radical and black feminism and get decent marks. The three women's studies students in Scenario 2.2 have a harder task debating the relationships between any of those feminisms and postmodernism. We will revisit their problem in Chapter 10.

Verdict

This chapter has not been about men and women in contemporary Britain, and so a verdict is not appropriate. What is clear, however, is that the intellectual climate in which to address sex roles is very different from 1893 or 1951.

Further reading

Abbott, P. and Wallace, C. (1990) *An Introduction to Sociology: Feminist Perspectives*. London: Routledge.
Lyon, D. (1999) *Postmodernity*, 2nd edn. Buckingham: Open University Press.

Part **two**
SOCIALIZATION *in a*
POST-INDUSTRIAL SOCIETY

Part two presents material on socialization from infancy to young adulthood. It explores whether child-rearing has changed, whether adolescents are living differently and whether young adults have been establishing themselves in their worlds over the past 30 years. Whether women have changed and men have not should be revealed in how children are reared, and in the lives of adolescents and young adults.

3 Gender *and the* post-industrial child

> The home must be guarded against sordid cares to the last possible moment; nothing upsets me more than the sight of those poor homes where wife and children are obliged to talk from morning to night of how the sorry earnings shall be laid out.
>
> (Gissing 1893/1980: 2)

In this quote, Dr Madden, a well-meaning but short-sighted man, is explaining how he sees the proper division of labour. The man works and takes all financial responsibilities; his wife and daughters are kept in ignorance of all 'sordid' topics, including money. In the novel, *The Odd Women*, he dies and leaves his three daughters destitute: a state they are particularly ill-fitted to meet because they have been reared in ignorance. For the past two centuries, there have been regular debates on how far children, especially girls, should be shielded inside the family from the horrors of the adult world.

In this chapter, the focus is on females and males who are aged up to 12 years, comparing them with people who were children in the 1890s and in the early 1950s. In each of the three periods, class differences are very marked. The lives of children in the upper and upper middle classes were, and are, very different from those in the working classes, especially in the poorest families or in orphanages. In the 1890s, compulsory elementary schooling for the working classes was 20 years old, although attendance was often poor, especially when children's labour was needed at home, on farms or where parents objected to the institution. Both sexes learnt basic literacy and numeracy, but girls also learnt sewing. In the upper and upper middle classes, young children of both sexes were taught at home, with boys more likely to go to school in the later stages of childhood. Girls were more likely to be kept entirely at home, with lessons from mother, a nursery governess, or in a domestic class with friends and neighbours. The girls' schools founded by feminists from the 1850s onwards (Delamont 1989) were still controversial and only used by more 'modern' or 'enlightened' families. The curriculum offered to the two sexes in childhood was less differentiated than that offered to adolescents. Middle- and upper middle-class boys were started on Latin and Greek at 6 or 7 years of age, a very different education from working-class children of either sex. Toys, games, books and clothing were strongly sex-differentiated in all classes, as were the 'ideals' of male and female behaviour and outlook (see Dyhouse 1981; Purvis 1989).

By the early 1950s, the school experiences of children were more similar across social classes, with middle-class girls usually attending school, and more similarities in the curricula. However, upper-class boys at preparatory schools still did Latin and Greek from the age of 6 or 7 years, unlike any other children. Parental ideals for young children were strongly gendered. In all social classes, parents wanted girls to be happy, clean and tidy, helpful and caring. The aims for boys were class-differentiated: the working classes wanted boys to be conformist and happy; the middle classes wanted autonomy, independence and happiness. (Neither class believed boys *could* be clean and tidy!) Clothing, toys, games, comics, books and the new media of radio, cinema and television were strongly gendered (see Newson and Newson 1965, 1970; Wilson 1980).

In this chapter, I explore the research on child-rearing (clothing, toys, socialization, early education) in the light of the changing nature of the family and the education system. I explore whether the experiences of girls and boys up to adolescence are similar to or different from the sexually stereotyped patterns of the first half of the century. If changes are found they will be explored in the light of the central question: Has the socialization of girls changed and that of boys not changed, or is that a myth? There has been a rapid expansion of literature on the sociology of childhood (Brannen and O'Brien 1996; Butler and Shaw 1996; Jenks 1996; James and Prout 1997). Much of this literature has focused on 'children' undifferentiated by sex, rather than replicating earlier work on sex differences and gender roles. Instead, major themes have been the importance of treating children as autonomous actors whose views should be treated seriously by researchers (Butler and Shaw 1996), sexuality (Jackson 1982) and the impact of adults' fears on children's lives (Scott *et al.* 1998). These are all important topics, but here I am most concerned to explore the gendered nature of childhood. Let us start in the university nursery at Kingsport.

Kingsport University 2005: Scene 3.1

It is a sunny March day in the university nursery. Mrs Pollin, the senior staff member in the toddlers section, separates George and Nat Brimsley who are fighting over a replica eighties motor car they have seized from Jill Jackson, to whom she returns it. George and Nat announce furiously, 'she can't have it, girls don't drive cars'. Jill retorts, 'I'm a doctor on the motorway, I drive to crashes', and as they run off George and Nat scream 'girls can't be doctors'. As Mrs Pollin comments to Miss Tremaine at coffee, this is a weird interaction. George and Nat's mother, Professor Brimsley, is the youngest professor of gynaecology in the UK, their paternal grandmother is also a doctor, yet they *still* claim women can't be doctors.

Throughout the last 30 years, many studies have shown pre-school children holding rigid sex stereotypes, even when their own families provide living counter-examples. For example, Lloyd and Duveen (1992: 10) found that 'the most sexist persons in a reception class are the children themselves'. Many of the stereotypes vanish later, but from everything we know the home and nursery environments of Nat, George and Jill are suffused with sex-role messages that stress difference and separations.

The child at home

In the early years of contemporary feminist social science, there were several pioneering – and revealing – studies of various aspects of child-rearing (see Delamont 1990). Although Anglo-Saxon parents believed, or told researchers they believed, that parents should treat boys and girls equally, the gendered nature of childhood was easily discovered by investigators. Whether one looked at names, clothing, toys bought, expenditure on presents, media images, language used to speak to children, adult interpretation of children's behaviour, play in schools, teacher expectations, teacher behaviour, content of school books or chaperonage, the research kept on coming up with a rhetoric of equality that masked or obscured a gender-stereotyped practice. Thus, parents spent the same amount of money on children's Christmas presents (equality) but deployed the money differently. Thus boys got a £200 mountain bike, while girls got clothes, furniture and other 'necessities' and smaller toys (a £60 dress, a £40 bean bag and a £100 doll's pram). Similarly, boys' toys encouraged spatial reasoning, adventurous role-play and geographical mobility (construction kit, Batman outfit, a bicycle), whereas girls' toys reinforced verbal reasoning, domestic role-play and staying close to home (books and a doll's house, Sindy's ballet dress and aerobics kit, the doll's pram).

Most of the research conducted in this area was done in the 1970s and early 1980s; equivalent studies have not been performed recently. However, a glance at any catalogue from any mail-order firm will show that children's worlds are still very gendered. The leaflets produced by Toys 'Я' Us divide boys' toys (focused on sport, violence and transport) from girls' toys (focused on domesticity, caretaking and dressing up). The clothing section of the *Marshall Ward* Winter Catalogue for 1999 illustrates the same pattern. Baby clothes come in four colours: there are two shades of pink (one pastel, one fuscia), two shades of blue (one pastel, one electric), green and lilac. The traditionalist can put the baby girl into a pastel pink suit, the modern parent can choose jade green. However, once the child is walking about, clothes become very sex-specific. Pyjamas are shown separately for boys and girls. Girls get pastel colours and their pyjamas are decorated with yawning cats, sleeping teddy bears, Minnie Mouse, hearts, more teddy bears, flowers and pink pigs. The boys' pyjamas are royal blue, jade green or scarlet, and show ghostbusters, Tom and Jerry, football club logos, Mickey Mouse and American football scenes.

Daytime clothing is also sex-differentiated, but less so than it was in the equivalent catalogues of the late 1970s. In 1999, there are tracksuits for both sexes and girls' clothes are more robust than a decade before. The clothing for 3- to 12-year-olds is more unisex, with the same jeans, cords, sweatshirts and tracksuits shown on boys and girls, although the boys are not modelling the lilac and pink versions. There are also separate clothing sections for boys and girls in which the boys wear dark-coloured tracksuits and pose with soccer balls, while the girls wear pastel shades and the few dresses that are to be found. However, in twelve pages only two show traditional frocks with frills. Whether that means mail-order girls' clothing was becoming less restrictive of movement, activity and dirt, or merely that 'fashion' that winter lacked frocks, was unclear.

The colour of clothing, especially for babies, may seem trivial. However, together with their names, the clothing of babies has been shown to have a great deal to do with how they are treated by adults. Walum (1977: 40) reported the results of an experiment in which mothers were shown Beth, a 6-month-old 'girl', in a frilly pink dress, and Adam, a 6-month-old 'boy' in blue rompers. Adults told 'Beth' she was beautiful and sweet, and chatted to her. In contrast, they threw 'Adam' up into the air, praised his strength and fierceness, and encouraged him to grasp things tightly. The catch was, as you will have guessed, that 'Beth' and 'Adam' were the same baby. It is easy to see, however, that faced with such interactive patterns from adults, that baby girls and baby boys will start to behave differently, long before they can speak.

In 1999, many adults are more comfortable when boy and girl children dress and play in different ways. Tomboys are tolerated, but deviation from a stereotyped male role causes concern in many adults. In the autumn of 1990, the *TV Times* problem page carried the following letter:

Is this little boy normal?
I'm very worried about a six-year-old boy in our family. His biggest pleasure is wearing skirts and his mother's shoes and putting on lipstick and nail polish. His parents are respected members of the church and I don't understand how they allow this. Is it normal behaviour or should something be done?

(*TV Times*, 18 November 1990)

Other such letters regularly appear in women's magazines. Take this letter, originally from the down-market tabloid *Daily Star*, reprinted in *New Statesman and Society* (16 October 1992):

My eight-year-old boy is a strange lad. He's bothered about the planet and interested in butterflies and insects as well as other animals. He never watches football. Do you think he's going to be gay?

(For further examples, see Delamont 1990: 12–14.) One of the biggest gaps in our knowledge is why British and, indeed, Anglo-Saxon culture is so scared of 'sissies' (see Connell 1987).

From birth, children are assigned to one or the other *gender* on the basis, usually, of their external sex organs. Then they are caught up in a torrent of myths, preconceptions and assumptions about what are 'natural', 'appropriate' and 'normal' things for males and females to do. The first piece of labelling that affects the newborn baby is the attribution of *gender*, although most people do not realize that this happens, because there is no general understanding of the different meaning of 'sex' and 'gender'.

Sex should only be used to cover things which are biologically based, such as chromosomes, hormones, gross anatomical differences and physiological features. Every other aspect of the differences between men and women, such as choice of clothing or leisure interests, is cultural and should be called *gender*. So a sex difference is the possession of an Adam's apple or a womb, while a liking for singing rugby songs or fine needlework is a gender difference.

Once the sex/gender label is applied, a complex process of labelling begins. The first part of this process is the giving of a name. Naming something is a way of gaining control over it, by fixing it firmly into a system of categories, a classification system, as Mary Douglas (1966) has shown us. The names given to children tell us quite a lot about them, including fixing them into a context, by religion, region and ethnic group. Mair and Eluned will be Welsh, Maeve and Siobhan Irish, Ishbel and Morag Scots, Montserrat from Catalonia and Raelene from Australia. Bernadette was probably raised Catholic, Hagar in the Jewish faith, Shanti in a Hindu family, Khadija in a Muslim one. Tiffany and Kylie are likely to be from working-class homes, while Eugenie and Perdita are middle- or upper-class names. In England and Wales in 1997, Jack and Chloe were the most popular names, and the fastest rising names were Courtney and Brandon (*Social Trends* 1999: 34). Names are strongly gendered, and boys suffer if they are given 'sissy' names. Boys are more likely to be given a monosyllabic name, like Jack (or one with a common monosyllabic abbreviation, such as David or Philip, which commonly go down to Dave and Phil). Girls are more likely to have a polysyllabic name, and there is more variety in girls' names.

Once Mair is dressed in pink floral leggings and given a Sindy doll, her experiences are diverging rapidly from an equivalent boy (let's call him Dyfrig), who wears navy blue cords and is given a Power Ranger. The toys children are given impact on their lives in one very practical way. Hart (1979) found that boys had much bigger territories than girls of similar ages partly because boys aged 9–12 years had bicycles, which increased their range, while girls did not. Boys also had a bigger territory because mothers operated a double standard. Boys had a range within which they were allowed to roam, plus a grey area beyond it where they played, their mothers knew they played, and nothing was said as long as they did not get too wet, dirty or damaged. Girls, on the other hand, had their permitted safe area strongly enforced.

In Britain during the 1950s and 1960s, girls were more closely chaperoned than boys of the same age and social class. Boys, especially working-class boys, were 'allowed' to play near roads, canals, rivers and building sites, because there were not enough 'safe' sites. One consequence of this was higher rates of mortality and injury among working-class boys than girls (Acheson 1998). The increased verbal skills in girls were thought to be developed by more social and, therefore, verbal interaction with adults. Middle-class parents exercised closer control over the physical location and playmates of their children than working-class parents, in part helped by owning homes with gardens.

There is evidence that children of both sexes aged 7–8 years were kept closer to adults in the 1990s than their parents were. Hillman *et al.* (1990) noted that whereas 80 per cent of 7- and 8-year-olds went to school alone in

1971, only 9 per cent were doing so in 1990. This is related to closure of neighbourhood schools, especially in rural areas, increased car ownership and parental fears about traffic accidents (a real danger) and violent attacks (a false one). Children are much more in danger of violence and sexual abuse inside their circle of relatives and friends than they are from 'strangers'. Children under one year of age are in the most danger; those between 5 and 15 the least. In the UK, 600 children die every year in accidents; about six are murdered. (The Dunblane shootings in 1996 were an exception, horrendous precisely because such incidents are rare in Britain.)

The discourse on risk and children analysed by Scott *et al.* (1998) is deeply confused. Parents are both warned to protect children *and* accused of molly-coddling them so they become couch potatoes; the media are attacked for forcing children into vicarious experiences of sex and violence which destroy their innocence; schools are subjected to a discourse of derision (Delamont 1999a).

Parents usually raise children to fit with the society that the parents know and understand, in particular influenced by their experience of the labour market. Some people set out consciously to break with conventions, but most unconsciously try to prepare their children for the 'real life' they know. Different social classes have different labour market experiences, value different things in their children and discipline them differently. Over the past 50 years, middle- and working-class households differed more in terms of boys' upbringing than they did girls' upbringing. Parents kept girls more closely confined (chaperonage), emphasized cleanliness, verbal skills and 'modesty' than boys. Families who had experienced industrial jobs for men tried to inculcate boys with conformity and steadiness, while middle- and upper-class families aimed to get boys to be autonomous and show individuality and initiative. As the traditional industrial labour market with its strong division of labour by sex has weakened, it is possible that the aims and practices of child-rearing are changing, but as yet there is no evidence of this. Whatever ideas parents have about proper male and female behaviour, children very quickly experience media images, a peer group and, by the age of 4, their first institution.

In contemporary Britain, there is a paradox surrounding child-rearing and gender. Bernstein (1971) suggested that it was useful to think of some families as positional and others as personal. In positional families, people's roles and power are based on the position they hold: young or old, male or female, wage earner or pensioner. Thus, in a positional family, 'father knows best', 'children should be seen and not heard', and so on. The family works because each person has a role fixed for them. The family is rule-governed and decisions are made by the more powerful office holders. In a personal family, each individual is seen as someone with rights, views and feelings that need to be discussed, balanced, weighed up and traded off. The end result may not be very different: if the father hates camping the family will not have a camping holiday, but the processes of deciding to go to a hotel in Spain will be different. Concerning gender in childhood, this means that, in positional families, conventional, traditional, stereotyped sex roles will be normal. In personal ones, the rights of the child to act in stereotyped ways will not be challenged because the child has a right to its choices. Thus in the same street one little girl (Elizabeth) may have a 'My Little Pony' set because her mother thinks it is a suitable toy for a girl, and another (Perdita) may have it although her mother thinks it is sexist, stereotyped and vulgar because Perdita is allowed to choose her own toys as an autonomous person. The difference will be that Perdita's mother feels guilty because Perdita has not 'chosen' either a boys' toy such as a Power Ranger or a police car, *or* a non-violent educational toy from the Early Learning Centre.

Schooldays and playmates

As soon as children join any social organization, such as a playgroup or a nursery school, they meet institutional and peer expectations on a sustained, everyday basis. These can be much more rigid about gender roles than anything a child has previously encountered or, if a home operates very rigid gender stereotypes, confusing.

The schooling of children up to 11 or 12 years in the UK is overwhelmingly in the hands of exhausted and overworked women (Menter *et al.* 1997). Nursery schools are staffed by women paid abysmally low wages; those who teach in infant and primary classes earn poor salaries. Few men teach children under 12; children meet women teachers. However, the head of the primary school is likely to be a man.

Most teachers hold stereotyped, determinist views of sex differences, believing males and females to be biologically distinct (for detailed citations on this point, see Coffey and Delamont 2000; Titus 2000), and the effects of such beliefs are conservative. The female pupil is likely to be viewed as naturally more compliant, more nurturing, more verbal and more dependent than male pupils. Teachers who believe boys are biologically superior are unlikely to spend time and trouble on developing scientific and mathematical prowess in girl pupils (for detailed references, see Delamont 1990: pp. 25–6). Believing phenomena to be natural has doubly conservative effects: not only are believers unlikely to try to change the phenomena, they also fear that attempts to tamper with the *status quo* will be damaging to individuals and the social fabric.

Ironically, some studies have reported teachers reinforcing the behaviours in girls that they dislike. Serbin's (1978) research showed nursery school teachers objecting to girls 'clinging' and keeping close to them. Yet, when observed, it became clear that girls could only get teacher attention and responses when physically close; unlike boys, who received teacher attention wherever they were in the nursery, girls beyond touching distance were ignored. Observations in the south-east of England in reception classes at two schools show teachers similarly trapped (Lloyd and Duveen 1992), as does Hilton's (1991) work on playgroup workers. These latter two studies found no evidence that Serbin's research was known to teachers of young children. Other studies of teachers (see Delamont 1990) and of recruits to the occupation (e.g. Sikes 1991) revealed an occupational group that was unaware of feminist perspectives and ideas of gender as socially constructed, and unconscious of the school's role in reinforcing conservative messages about sex roles. Smithers and Zientek (1991) surveyed 219 infant teachers, 84 per cent of whom said that they tried to encourage both sexes to try activities traditionally associated with the other sex. The introduction of the National Curriculum in England in 1988 was also thought to have potential for lessening gender stereotyping by 63 per cent of the respondents. However, these data reflect what teachers said, not what they did. Observational research by Renold (1999, 2000) found little difference in classroom practices from a study conducted by Clarricoates (1987) 15 years earlier. The gender regimes of primary schools do differ according to their catchment area: in more middle-class schools, there is less traditional sex stereotyping.

It is easy to blame teachers for the conservative and conformist sex roles routinely reported from schools. However, teachers who wish to challenge conventional male and female behaviour, dress or speech patterns can find themselves pilloried by colleagues and facing resistance from pupils, who can be upset and angered by such challenges. Pupils' adherence to stereotyped sex roles is one striking finding of the research on pupils and gender which needs reiteration here. Study after study has shown that there is a triple standard in operation as far as children's and adolescents' sex stereotyping is concerned. Children and teenagers are relatively relaxed about their own gender-related behaviours, relatively stereotyped about same-sex peers and highly rigid about opposite-sex peers. Thus Tom believes it is fine for him to learn ballet, dubious for Philip to want to be a nurse and outrageous for Mandy to aim for veterinary medicine. Mandy feels confident that she can be a vet, doubts whether Pauline should strip down motorbikes as a hobby, and is sure Philip should not be a nurse and Tom should not learn ballet.

Such beliefs were reported by many of the respondents to the survey by Smithers and Zientek (1991). As one teacher reported: 'Boys never turn round and say that boys can't do cooking when we have cooking activities but they turn round and say that girls can't play with the Lego with them, or girls can't play with cars' (p. 12). In mixed schools, although boys and girls are taught in the same rooms and spend their leisure time in the same playgrounds, there is evidence that males and females avoid each other. Pupils do not sit together or work together unless a teacher forces them to do so (Delamont 1990: 38–40; Thorne 1993). The features of pupils' culture that led to this avoidance have been most sympathetically described by Raphaela Best (1983). She followed a cohort of pupils through childhood and into adolescence, learning about their culture and simultaneously confronting them with the illogicalities in their sex-role stereotypes. Her central argument is that schools teach children three curricula – one overt, two hidden. The academic curriculum and the official school rules are manifest, but behind them – and largely invisible to adults – were the rules of appropriate male and female behaviour learnt from peers and enforced by them. Concealed behind that first 'hidden' curriculum and the stereotyped peer culture was a third, even more secret children's culture, where sexuality and obscenity were crucial. The third area was the most carefully hidden from adults. As Bauman (1982: 178) explains:

The free peer group activity of children is by its very nature a privileged realm in which adults are alien intruders, especially so insofar as much of the childhood folklore repertoire violates what children understand to be adult standards of decorum.

This 'hidden' third curriculum is the most savagely sexist. Here boys are taunted as 'poofs' for wearing the 'wrong' shirt or carrying the wrong lunch box, girls are 'slags' for their choice of hairstyle or 'lesbians' for getting their sums correct. Because in this realm there is a great deal of sexual and obscene language, few researchers are able to study it, and it is not possible for teachers or parents to address the sexism that permeates it.

Fine (1987: 238–40) reported the complex process of getting pre-adolescent boys to trust him with the vulgar-obscene aspects of their culture, as did Canaan (1986) and Measor (1989). (Working to change boys is discussed in Askew and Ross 1988.) The conservative perspective on gender held by pre-adolescent pupils shows up in the research on scary stories told before transfer to secondary school (Measor and Woods 1984; Delamont 1991; Pugsley *et al.* 1996). Researchers can gradually gain access to the pupils' world if, like Best, they reveal themselves to be unshockable and trustworthy. Britain has no study as rich as that of Best, although Clarricoates (1987), Connolly (1998) and Renold (1999) are sensitive to the secret lives of children.

Verdict

There is no evidence that the lives of pre-adolescent children have changed over the past 50 years except for the greater chaperonage of both sexes. Class gaps in illness, accidents and early death have not closed; sex stereotyping is still fierce, especially inside the children's own peer culture; and girls perform better at school, especially in verbal subjects. However, if we look back to 1893, the lives of children are very different because life expectancy is much greater and families much smaller. Sex differentiation in the beliefs of families are less, although behaviour may not have changed as much.

Further reading

For an eye-opening study of children in Britain, see Lloyd, B. and Duveen, G. (1992) *Gender Identities and Education.* London: Harvester Wheatsheaf.
To see what sociologists of childhood are doing, see James, A. and Prout, A. (eds) (1997) *Constructing and Reconstructing Childhood.* London: Falmer Press.
For an ethnography of two primary schools, see Connolly, P. (1998) *Racism, Gender Identities and Young Children.* London: Routledge.
On the 1890s, see Dyhouse, C. (1981) *Girls Growing Up in Victorian and Edwardian England.* London: Routledge & Kegan Paul.
On the 1950s, see Newson, J. and Newson, E. (1970) *Four Years Old in an Urban Community.* Harmondsworth: Penguin.

4 Gender *and the* post-industrial adolescent

> The atmosphere of the house was intellectual . . . but it never occurred to Dr Madden that his daughters would do well to study with a profes-sional object . . . the thought . . . of his girls having to work for money was so utterly repulsive to him that he could never seriously dwell upon it.
>
> (Gissing 1893/1980: 3)

When Gissing wrote *The Odd Women*, the idea that young women should be educated so that they could enter an occupation was a novel one, regarded as repulsive by many families. Where adolescent girls received any education, it was usually sharply different from that given to equivalent boys (Delamont 1989). Since the 1870s, the education of adolescents has become more sim-ilar and is more likely to take place in co-educational institutions. However, this does not mean that the lives of adolescents are necessarily similar.

In this chapter, the focus is on females and males aged 12–19 years, comparing them with people who were adolescents in the 1890s and in the early 1950s. The chapter explores the empirical evidence on adolescent lives (education, sexual orientation and peer group adherence). In the light of the evidence, two central questions will be explored. First, whether adolescence was a product of the industrial revolution, which has been rendered obsolete by post-industrialism. Second, whether the roles of males and females today in adolescence are similar to, or different from, those of the first half of the century. If the evidence suggests that female roles have changed while those of males have not, the reasons for this need to be explored. If it is a myth, the reasons for the plausibility of the myth will be explored. There is an excellent body of literature on adolescent masculinity (e.g. Mac an Ghaill 1994) that is central to this chapter.

At the level of individual young people, there are tensions around sex roles and gender equality, which are embodied and enacted in their homes, schools and leisure activities.

Kingsport University 2005: Scene 4.1

Dr Ross Crossfield, a chemist, is cooking supper for his two teenagers, Tamsin aged 13 and Dermot aged 15. Both are complaining that

their mother, Dr Ursula Crossfield, head of gender studies, had
made them a laughing stock at school. A book she has published,
on gender ideologies in business and management studies courses,
especially their texts and examination papers, was featured in the
Times Educational Supplement and picked up for mockery in *The
Daily Telegraph* and *The Sun*. Teachers and fellow pupils have
been ridiculing them: they are, they claim, so embarrassed by her
behaviour that they can't face their friends. She, they contend, has
no idea what it is like to attend a modern comprehensive school.

Adolescence, as we have known it in the twentieth century, was an
invention of modernity, or at least of industrialization. Once people who had
physically adult bodies but no skills were not required by the labour market
and, therefore, could not support new households until they had had an
extended education, a new category of person – the adolescent – was born.
When the pioneer psychologist G. Stanley Hall produced his two-volume,
1800-page blockbuster on *Adolescence* in 1905, the new research category was
reified. The Freudian theories about sexual identity and sexuality in Hall's book
reinforced the economic determinism of extended education and dependency. One of the uncertainties we face is whether the category will vanish
with the industrial era.

In the 1890s, class differences were very strong in adolescence. Many
working-class teenagers of both sexes were in full-time employment by the age
of 14 and nearly all of them were by the age of 16. Secondary education was
restricted to those whose parents could pay, with the small number of schol-
arships being for boys. Working-class girls who aspired to enter teaching did
so as pupil teachers, being paid to work as they trained. Middle- and upper-
class adolescents were still dependent on their families: the boys in education, the girls either in education or at home. Segregation of the sexes was
very strict in the middle and upper classes between puberty and marriage.
The curriculum and the leisure pursuits of the two sexes in these classes were
very different (see Dyhouse 1981; Purvis 1989).

By the 1950s, two world wars had changed the nation's ideas about the
need for an educated labour force. Secondary education for both sexes had
been made free and compulsory in 1944. State secondary education was sex-
differentiated, with girls offered less science, no technology and forced into
cookery, needlework and laundry lessons. The ideological climate was en-
shrined in several government reports that stressed a domestic destiny for
girls that needed to permeate their schooling (Wolpe 1974). Only the minority of young women who attended the highly academic grammar and independent schools got a high status male curriculum of Latin and physics
(Delamont 1989). As Wilson (1980) shows, the early 1950s were an era of
strong sex segregation in adolescence.

Although the adults who plan schooling no longer espouse the strong
sex segregation in curricula and disciplinary regimes of the 1950s (Heron
1990), adolescents do not necessarily feel themselves to be living in an
egalitarian world. The sociological research of the 1980s and 1990s found
that teenagers such as Tamsin and Dermot experience their secondary school

as strongly sex-stereotyped and hostile to anti-sexist ideas. After an analysis of educational experience, the role of peer groups, media and other influences is covered. If we begin with Tamsin, we can look at the experiences of girls in the comprehensive secondary school in terms of the body and the self, the curriculum, school regimes, peer pressures and academic achievement. Dermot's experiences will follow. I demonstrate that class differences are increasingly apparent in adolescence, before addressing problems that arise when attempts are made to challenge the sexist regimes of schools.

Teenage girls and the contested body

Frank (1990, 1991) argued that sociology had fallen behind other spheres of academic discourse because sociologists were neglecting to afford 'centrality to the body'. After these justified criticisms were made in the early 1990s, the discipline began to pay serious attention to the body (see Scott and Morgan 1993; Holland and Adkins 1996). Certainly, the school world of Tamsin Crossfield needs to be understood as an intellectual and social institution in which the bodies of young women are displayed.

For adolescent girls in industrial societies, the body is a central concern. Consider the following letter published in the magazine *Woman*:

They tease me
Last week I was on the school bus, and some boys in my class stole my bag. Before I could stop them, they'd opened the side pocket and found my tampons. I just burst into tears and got off at the next stop. Now they all laugh and tease me, calling me names like Little Miss Tampon. Please help me. I hate school and sometimes I want to kill myself.

(*Woman*, 3 July 1989)

A decade later, nothing had changed. *Mizz* published the following:

I am too frightened to do PE since I started my periods about three months ago. I don't want to use period pads in case people see them in the class, and I'm too worried to use tampons. My mum said you can lose tampons inside you and they can give you cancer. What should I do?

(*Mizz*, 11 August 1999)

If this seems like two hysterical young women, it is actually a public manifestation of sexual harassment in and around schools (Herbert 1989), as well as a specific problem about a bodily function. Prendergast (1989) details problems facing girls' management of menstruation in school. The National Child Development Study of 12,000 girls born in 1958 found that 75 per cent of them were menstruating by the age of 13. At the age of 16, 36 per cent had painful menstruation, but only 3 per cent had consulted a doctor (Fogelman 1976). For some ethnic and religious minorities, including gypsies, a girl's first menstruation is a signal to remove her from the company of males outside her family (Jeffery 1976; Okely 1983), including removal from co-education.

Menstruation is the private aspect of the other bodily changes affecting adolescent girls. Paechter (1998) discusses other aspects of adolescent girls' subjection to the hegemonic male gaze in school. The role of the body in the lives of girls at comprehensive school can be illustrated from data collected at Melin Court School in Coalthorpe, a city in the north of England (Delamont and Galton 1986), especially the 'leotard lesson' (Delamont 1998). This is an analysis of a physical education (PE) lesson for forty girls in their first week at a mixed comprehensive, where the girls were taken through the kit they needed, the sports they would learn and an agenda of appropriate female behaviour. The lesson is clearly focused on 'those doggedly fleshy, troubling matters of female embodiment' as Hughes and Witz (1997: 56) characterize them. The leotard lesson displays discourse about four ways in which the adolescent body is to be disciplined (and in which the physical education teachers' bodies are already disciplined), which are embodiments of the four dimensions of the disciplined body outlined by Frank (1991).

We can trace male hegemony through the lesson, especially the teachers' discourse. In the opening moments, the girls are warned that they must dress modestly in 'decent knickers' or a leotard because of the gaze of the boys. Miss Sugnett warns: 'If you don't wear a leotard you must buy decent knickers because of the boys on the top field' (cf. Mahony 1985; Wolpe 1988; Herbert 1989).

> The lesson moved on to showers and swimming. For swimming they need a swimsuit. (There was no uniform swimsuit. Girls could wear whatever costume they owned.) The PE teachers keep a record of who has a shower and who goes swimming, when you are 'on period' they put 'O' on the record. If you cannot swim you go to the baths, but tell the swimming master you're 'on period'. The girls were reassured: 'he won't be embarrassed, he's a married man'.
>
> (Delamont, field notes)

The menstrual calendars of the girls are to be scrutinized not only by the female physical education teacher, but also by the man at the swimming pool. In this lesson, the teachers stress the inevitability of biology/anatomy as destiny, in ways that reflect the patriarchal discourse of female bodies as flawed and limiting. The teachers appear fixated on modesty, menstruation, marriage and pregnancy. Pregnancy appears in the discourse as a time when one's fingers swell.

> No jewellery – at the beginning of the lesson they must put it in the jewellery box – no jewellery to be worn during PE – 'except sleepers'. One girl says she 'can't get this ring off – it's too tight to come off'. She has had it on since she was a baby. The teachers say immediately 'tight rings are dangerous'. They talk of how tight rings can cut off the circulation 'when your fingers swell when you're pregnant'. The girls are told to get tight rings cut off, because they are dangerous. Failing that they should use soap to ease them off, or cover them with sticking plaster during PE lessons.
>
> (Delamont, field notes)

Then the girls once again get the warnings about disguising underwear and menstruation (again without any mention of tampons as an alternative to bulky 'Dr White's).

> One girl has brought some shorts instead of the skirt which Miss Sugnett says are fine to start off with, but 'We'd prefer you not to wear just shorts on their own', because girls 'get fatter as you get older and a skirt will cover your Dr. White's better'.

(Delamont, field notes)

Given these data (see Delamont 1998; Herbert 1989; Prendergast 1989; Paechter 1998), the letters to the problem pages no longer seem hysterical: they sound just like the respondents in research studies. Our fictional, middle-class, adolescent Tamsin may not have had her tampons stolen and displayed. However, her body will still be subject to the hegemonic gaze of the males in her school, because that is an experience common to women in all social classes (Measor 1989).

Schools as social arenas

Inside the secondary school, young women like Tamsin not only have to manage their own bodies, but also their social relations with teachers and with peers. The research on interactions between adolescent girls and their teachers is limited, contentious (see Delamont 1990, 1996; Woods and Hammersley 1993; Paechter 1998) and has been overtaken in importance by a 'great leap forward' in young women's school achievement. While feminist researchers were bemoaning the sexist nature of secondary schooling (e.g. Delamont 1990; Measor and Sikes 1992), which was blamed for the under-achievement of girls in them, the next generations of women began to out-perform boys (Fewell and Patterson 1990; Turner *et al.* 1995; Arnot *et al.* 1996, 1999; Salisbury 1996; Salisbury and Riddell 2000) at 16 and at 18 in almost all subjects. The young women studied by Mac an Ghaill (1994) may have experienced schools as sexist, but it no longer depressed their academic achievements below those of the boys in the same schools.

Young women, like Tamsin, are likely to meet teachers who believe the sexes are biologically unequal and different, who focus on boys in their classroom strategies because disorder results if they do not, and who hold negative stereotypes of adolescent females as hard working but dull and prone to giggles and 'silliness' (for a full review of the research on these points, see Coffey and Delamont 2000). Of course, there are teachers and schools committed to equality of treatment, and parents like the Crossfields will have looked for a school that encouraged girls to do sciences, perhaps by having single-sex classes in information technology, maths and science, or other strategies. In the terminology used by Gewirtz *et al.* (1995), who have done careful research on how and why parents in different social classes choose secondary schools for their children, the Crossfields, as middle-class intellectuals, are skilled choosers and sex equality would be an important dimension of schooling.

It is clear, however, that school teaching is not an occupation where either the ideals or the practice of sex equality, far less of feminism, have been adopted. Feminist ideas are not widely taught to student teachers (Coffey and Acker 1992; Titus 2000) and are not commonly held by practitioners (see Coffey and Delamont 2000). When teachers are concerned about sex equality, it is likely to be an issue in the staffroom regarding pay or promotion, rather than an ideology that has permeated classroom practices. This was certainly the case for the women teachers at Parnell School (Mac an Ghaill 1994), who complained that the school was suffused with unrecognized masculine hegemonic practices under a rhetoric of equality. The research reported in Epstein *et al.* (1998) and Salisbury and Riddell (2000) came to the same conclusions. Despite media stories (see Delamont 1999), adolescents do not meet teachers who operate as feminists, or schools that are run to favour girls. For Tamsin and, indeed, all adolescent girls, the lived reality of everyday school life is dependent on the peer group, perhaps even more than the teachers. At Parnell School, Mac an Ghaill (1994) found the female pupils tried to balance housework, schoolwork and male oppression, while they attempted to avoid attracting three negative labels from their classmates: it was hard not to be a 'slag', a 'lezzie' or 'really snobby'. Avoiding all three left little breathing space and Tamsin would have similar problems. Central to school life are peer pressures.

Same-sex pupil relations

Young women at school place a high value on their same-sex friends. In *Jackie* for 25 May 1991, the problem page carried eleven problems, four of which concerned relationships with female friends. One girl complains her friend is nice when they are alone but horrid when others are present; one fears her long-standing relationship with her best friend is breaking down; a third has one friend who is unpopular with her other 'mates'; the fourth suffers because her friends think she is too well behaved in her school where her father is head of year. *Shout's* summer special in August 1999 similarly carried a double-page spread of problems about female friends. 'Nadia' has lost her friend because she reached puberty later; another girl's friend has become obsessed with hanging around boys; two others have fallen out with a person who had been their friend since childhood; a fifth worries about losing her friends when they go to secondary school. The coordinators of the problem pages in all the teenage magazines report a similar bias in the letters that they receive: relationships with same-sex peers matter a great deal to young women.

The research by social scientists has reported a similar preoccupation. The centrality of the female friendship group to school life has been reported for more than 20 years. Lambart (1976, 1982), Llewellyn (1980), Meyenn (1980) and Delamont (1989) all found girls' peer groups in school during the 1960s and 1970s which functioned as important parts of their members' lives and mediated school experience through group attitudes. Nilan (1991) researched the moral order of two cliques, one in a middle-class Sydney school and one in a more working-class rural Catholic school in New South Wales. In both contexts, survival in a friendship group depended on 'fairness', 'honesty' and on 'obligation to show caring' and, in both settings, the maintenance of the friendships was extremely significant to the young women. In the UK, the most empathetic recent study of such female friendships is that by Hey (1997).

The interaction between the girls in any particular friendship group can be important for the academic involvement and achievement of all its members. Solomon (1991) followed a group of 11- and 12-year-old girls through their first months of science. One clique – Karen, Sheila, Mary and Anna – begins science with Karen very keen on the subject. Within 2 months the whole quartet have 'decided' that girls hate science, are not good at it and Karen has abandoned her original position. In such groups, life chances are shaped (see also Measor 1984).

Given the nature of secondary schooling in the UK, the academic achievements of young women, which have risen sharply over the past 30 years, are surprising. Scholars are unclear about the reasons for the marked improvement in girls' school performance, which has been apparent in Northern Ireland, Scotland, Wales and England. The achievements of girls have equalled those of boys since the late 1970s, although this went unnoticed by the media until the mid-1990s (Delamont 1999, 2000a). As Northern Ireland still has an eleven-plus examination and grammar schools, it cannot be a consequence of the comprehensive school, and there is no evidence that school processes have changed. Although adolescent girls from middle-class homes are more successful than those from working-class homes, achievement has risen throughout the century, in particular since 1944 when secondary education became compulsory for both sexes. It is likely that this is due to young women recognizing that the labour market now offers very few jobs for female school leavers without qualifications.

The current position of boys is very different. If we turn to Dermot's world, we enter the sphere of a full-blown moral panic.

Dermot's world

If the secondary comprehensive school is experienced by Tamsin as sexist, but as an arena where girls are more academically successful, how does Dermot see, feel and think about it? In the 1990s, boys have been the subject of a moral panic: a myth that boys are 'failing' in British schools (Epstein *et al.* 1998). In fact, of course, not all boys are failing in school: the category 'boy' needs to be disaggregated.

There is a 40-year tradition of empirical research on the lives of boys in secondary schools (Delamont 2000a), which carefully differentiated young men by class and by their responses to schooling. In general, boys from middle-class families were shown to succeed in school and stay on longer, while those from the working class left earlier and achieved less (Halsey *et al.* 1980). However, case studies in particular schools showed that the internal organization of the school, especially whether it had streaming, could 'create' successful working-class pupils who adopted middle-class attitudes and groups of anti-school boys who rejected everything the institution had to offer. These studies spanned the coming of the comprehensive school, for the early ones were done in grammar and secondary modern schools (or in senior and junior secondaries in Scotland), whereas the later ones were conducted in comprehensives.

Re-reading these studies in the light of the contemporary moral panic about 'failing boys', two things are apparent. First, the type of boy who fails, or chooses to reject the school, has been strikingly consistent from Hargreaves (1967) through Willis (1977) and Brown (1987) to Mac an Ghaill (1994) and Sewell (1998, 1999), an argument explored elsewhere (Delamont 1999, 2000a). Second, there was a lack of attention to issues of masculinity and sexuality in the earlier work. When Hargreaves (1967) and Lacey (1970) contrasted pro- and anti-school subcultures in streamed boys' schools in the 1960s, they chronicled two male responses to schooling, but did not discuss them in terms of masculinity. Those boys who did not fit either of the two main subcultures were not discussed in any detail, but were treated as 'isolates' and 'misfits'. The school ethnographies of the 1980s (Ball 1980; Burgess 1983; Beynon 1985; Brown 1987) were much more sensitive to gender. However, these investigators did not treat masculinity – either their own or that of male pupils – as problematic. Only with the studies of Aggleton (1987) and Abraham (1989a, 1989b, 1995) did male researchers begin to treat their own masculinity and that of their male respondents as a research topic in its own right.

Mac an Ghaill (1994) is central to this new wave of attention to masculinity. At Parnell School, in the English Midlands, where he did fieldwork between 1990 and 1992, the central actors are four sets of boys: the Real Englishmen, the New Enterprisers, the Academic Achievers and the Macho Lads. As Parnell served a catchment area mixed in class and race terms, it was an ideal research site for Mac an Ghaill to explore the complexities of masculinity. He drew on the Australian study of R.W. Connell and his colleagues (1982), which was the first attempt to explore how adolescents' school careers have to be understood in the context of class, gender and race. At Parnell, the four types of boy are wrestling to achieve adult masculinity in a city without any traditional manual male employment.

Mac an Ghaill's (1994) Macho Lads and Academic Achievers are nineties versions of the male responses to schooling seen in previous generations, like the polarized anti-school and pro-school boys at Lumley Secondary Modern in the 1960s (Hargreaves 1967), and the lads and earholes of Hammertown Secondary Modern (Willis 1977) or their equivalents at Downtown boys' secondary modern (Hammersley 1977, 1980) and Victoria Road Comprehensive in the 1970s (Beynon 1985). British schools have polarized those who conform to the rules, do their schoolwork and succeed *versus* those who break the rules, avoid schoolwork and leave unqualified for at least 50 years. Here Parnell School is typical of many British state schools and, therefore, we can imagine that Dermot and Tamsin's Kingsport comprehensive is essentially similar. Dermot, given his family background, is likely to be an Academic Achiever, who knows only too well that the Macho Lads think he is a 'girl', a 'poof', not a proper male at all. As long as they do not assault him physically, he can ignore them, because he knows he is going to have a more economically secure life.

Mac an Ghaill's (1994) research is most interesting for its discovery of two other lifestyles at Parnell. The New Enterprisers and the Real Englishmen are varieties of male pupil response to schooling which had not previously been reported by sociologists of education. The New Enterprisers are 'CTC wannabes' (that is they would have preferred to attend a City Technology College; Walford and Miller 1991), clearly Thatcher's children (see Pilcher and Wagg 1996) and make a fascinating read. They have plunged into new subjects such as IT (information technology) and business studies, believing these are the keys to employment. Unlike the Macho Lads, who believe there are no longer any jobs, the New Enterprisers have listened to their fathers. As Wayne told Mac an Ghaill:

> A lot of kids in the low classes say that there are no jobs, but my dad has become self-employed. He says there's jobs for people but they have to get out and find them ... You don't want to be working for someone else all your life when you can make more money yourself.
>
> (Mac an Ghaill 1994: 72)

These boys resented the disruptive behaviour of the Macho Lads and those teachers who tried to get them to work on old-fashioned academic subjects.

Given two parents who teach in the university, Dermot is likely to be successful in school, to be an Academic Achiever. University staff produce children who do better in the British education system than those from any other family background (Heath 1981). However, a boy from a liberal middle-class home who was rejecting the school, like those studied by Aggleton (1987), can face particular problems in establishing a secure male identity.

If Dermot is failing in his schoolwork – if he is not in the top class heading for ten GCSEs and the sixth form – he might be a typical recruit for a friendship group such as Mac an Ghaill's Real Englishmen. Unlike the other three categories, the Real Englishmen were an all-white group, and their label was one they pinned on themselves. They told Mac an Ghaill:

> *Thomas:* We were fooling around one night, talking about our parents and all the crap liberal stuff that they talk about all the time. And someone just said 'they can believe whatever the fuck they want, we're real men'.
>
> *Ben:* We just call ourselves the REMs, rapid eye movement. Pretty Cool, yeah? We're living in a fantasy world away from the heavy issues.
>
> (Mac an Ghaill 1994: 79)

In addition to being 'real men' rejecting their fathers' 'anti-sexism', these boys were anxious to have an ethnic identity:

> *Adam:* It's like we can't be English – be proud of being English ... all the Asian and the black kids, they can be Asian or black. They can be proud of their countries ... we're not talking about colour. We're talking about culture.
>
> (Mac an Ghaill 1994: 84)

These boys complained that their parents – liberal new middle-class professionals – had adopted anti-sexist and anti-racist positions, which did not fit the reality of the teenagers' experiences in a co-educational multi-racial comprehensive. The second way in which the REMs were interesting is their attachment to 'English' culture. Mac an Ghaill contrasts this with an Irish identity held by other 'white' boys in the school. There is an urgent need for work on male identity and different varieties of Britishness, a theme revisited in Chapter 6.

Dermot Crossfield might well be feeling similar frustrations if he were failing to achieve good academic results. The REMs were celebrating an anti-feminist, 'real' manhood coupled with a right-wing English nationalism. Research in schools in the last 20 years has also found a few young men choosing to rebel against their schools by embracing a flamboyant androgyny (wearing make-up and effeminate clothes, mincing, studying needlework arts and drama). If Dermot found the gender regime of his school oppressive and was rebelling against the 10 GCSE conformity of the top class, he might have adopted an anti-Macho anti-school stance like the Gothic Punks stud-ied by John Abraham (1989a, 1989b, 1995) and the Spatown Rebels studied by Aggleton (1987). Abraham found that boys who were anti-school, but not in the conventional macho, laddish way teachers expected, were ferociously unpopular with male staff.

The peer group and the friendship group are just as important for boys as for girls, but the dynamics inside them appear to be different. Male groups seem to be more competitive and less intimate. Boys interviewed deny that they could admit vulnerabilities and problems to their male friends: secrets would not be kept, weaknesses once exposed would later be used against you. Holland *et al.* (1998: 161) show how 'The peer group plays an important part in young men's progress towards "appropriate" masculinity'. One activ-ity in the peer group is the telling of sexual 'performance stories', which separate 'wimps' from 'gladiators': 'Performance stories function to establish a young man's position in the competition' (Holland *et al.* 1998: 161). Many young men, when talking to women investigators, recognize that perform-ance stories are often lies, and that the male sexuality they embody is a crude, mechanistic and sexist one, but it is still powerful and constraining. As I show later, that version of sexuality is constraining for both sexes.

Boys in academic bands, succeeding in school, are scorned by anti-school boys for being wimps rather than gladiators. The contemporary moral panic about failing boys ignores the existence of groups such as Mac an Ghaill's (1994) Academic Achievers and New Entrepreneurs, focusing instead on the REMs and the Macho Lads (Epstein *et al.* 1998; Arnot *et al.* 1999; Salisbury and Riddell 2000). In fact, the academic achievement of boys in all four nations of the UK has risen consistently over the past 30 years: far more young men from all social classes achieve credentials, stay on at school after the legal leaving age and proceed to post-compulsory education now than at any time in the past.

The minority of boys, from unskilled working-class homes and includ-ing too many African Caribbeans (Sewell 1997, 1999), who reject schooling for the lifestyle of the 'Macho Lad' are a long-standing problem for schools, and have only become a *cause célèbre* because of the improved performance of girls. We need to be careful not to be swept away by a moral panic about 'failing', anti-school, working-class boys. This is not a new problem (Delamont 1999). Geoff Pearson's (1983) historical study of recurrent moral panics about hooliganism shows that the upper and middle classes have been worried about the 'threat' from anti-school working-class boys since at least 1680. Such boys are a social and educational problem, but not a new phenomenon (Delamont 2000a).

The Status Zero trajectory

Tamsin and Dermot are middle-class adolescents attending school and living in an intact family. Their worst problems are embarrassing liberal parents, spots and peer pressures. Many adolescents have much more serious problems – poverty, racism, domestic violence, and so on. A minority of young adults 'vanish' from official Britain into what Rees *et al.* (1996) called 'Status Zero'. (This term and their research are addressed in the next chapter.) The most unfortunate adolescents are already embarked on a trajectory into Status Zero by the age of 13 or 14. Adolescents truanting from school, in care, involved in substance misuse, or victims of sexual abuse or domestic violence, are likely to end up unqualified and unemployable, which can make them socially excluded by the age of 16 or 17.

Between comfortable adolescents like Tamsin and Dermot, and those sliding into Status Zero, class inequalities bite hard in adolescence. Poverty and social class lead to pupils being in different schools and achieving much less in terms of credentials.

The world beyond school

Thus far the chapter has concentrated on the school lives of adolescents. This reflects the balance of the research and the vital role school plays in determining adult life. However, there are four other spheres in which adolescents operate: the family, paid employment, leisure and the search for a sexual identity.

In adolescence, the sexual double standard becomes an important element in male–female relationships. Paul Willis (1977: 43–6) stressed the sexist nature of the beliefs about women held by the 'lads' he studied in Hammertown. They operated a double standard between the steady girlfriend (virtuous and sexually faithful) and the 'easy lay' (cheap and promiscuous). These young men seemed to believe that sexual experience was addictive for young women. One of his informants claimed that 'once they've had it, they want it all the time, no matter who it's with' so that the 'easy lay' is damned by the whole group. Willis suggests the girls have no scope to be assertive or sexual and are forced into romantic silliness. This double standard was clearly recognized by the girls studied by Deidre Wilson (1978), Lesley Smith (1978) and Sue Lees (1986). Wilson's sample of young women aged 13–15 years in northern England divided girls into virgins, 'nice' girls who only had sex when in love with a steady, responsible boy, and 'lays' who were promiscuous and had sex with anyone and everyone. Virgins and nice girls avoided being friends with, or even being seen with, 'lays' because association with a bad girl could tarnish their own reputation. Lesley Smith's sample of 14- to 16-year-olds in Bristol held similar views, even when they doubted the justice of them. For example:

> *Liz:* Look I don't believe there should be one standard for a boy and another for a girl. But there just is round here and there's not much you can do about it. A chap's going to look for someone who hasn't had it off with every bloke. So as soon as you let him put a leg over you, you've got a bad name.
>
> (Smith 1978: 83)

Similarly, Sue Lees was told a decade later:

> When there're boys talking and you've been out with more than two you're known as the crisps that they're passing around . . . The boy's alright but the girl's a bit of scum.
>
> (Lees 1986: 40)

Adolescent girls are careful to maintain their reputation as 'nice' girls and avoid being labelled 'slags' and 'sluts'. The latter can be spotted by a variety of signs, but one of them, in the boys' eyes, is a girl's knowledge and use of contraception. In mixed schools, girls spend considerable time and energy avoiding behaving *either* as too clever and hard working *or* as a slut. There is not much space between the two negative roles (Fine 1998).

Thirty years have passed since the work of Smith and Wilson was published, but subsequent studies such as that of Holland *et al.* (1998) suggest little has changed. Many young women are sexually active before the legal age of consent (16 years). Although sexuality and sexual orientation are discussed in more detail in the chapter on young adults, one point is important here. Holland *et al.* (1998: 11) found the double standard alive and well:

> Behaviour that made him successfully masculine, a real man, caused her to lose her reputation – to be seen as loose, slack, a slag – a reputation policed just as forcibly by women as by men . . . Young women could be seen playing an active role in constituting and reproducing male dominance.

Verdict

Is there evidence of females changing and males not in contemporary adolescence? In school achievement, young women have certainly improved their performance to equal that of young men. In terms of aspirations, attitudes to sex roles and participation in social life, the evidence is not convincing. Most sex differences in adolescence seem to be as old as industrialization, and are overshadowed by class differences and problems linked to poverty.

Further reading

Epstein, D., Elwood, J., Hey, V. and Maw, J. (eds) (1998) *Failing Boys?* Buckingham: Open University Press.

Pilcher, J. and Wagg, S. (eds) (1996) *Thatcher's Children*. London: Falmer Press.

On the 1890s, see Dyhouse, C. (1981) *Girls Growing Up in Victorian and Edwardian England*. London: Routledge & Kegan Paul.

On the 1950s, see Heron, L. (ed.) (1990) *Truth, Dare or Promise?* London: Virago.

5 Gender *and* young adulthood

> It is your work to train and encourage girls in a path as far as possible from that of a husband-hunter. Let them marry later, if they must . . . you will have taught them that marriage is an alliance of intellects, not a means of support.
>
> (Gissing 1893/1980: 58)

In this quote, Rhoda Nunn, one of the heroines of the novel, is arguing that women need to be able to earn their own living to develop rationality, so if they wish to marry they can do so for good motives, not from desperation or because they are blinded by romantic sentimentality, due to reading too many frivolous novels.

The focus of this chapter is gender roles between the ages of 16 and 25 years. This is when class differences in labour market entry, and in the establishment of 'adult' sex roles centred on marriage/cohabitation/parenthood/leaving the parental home, are at their most extreme. The evidence on sex roles in this age range is scrutinized to explore the central issue, have women's roles changed and men's remained the same? Many of the issues raised here are explored in more detail in Furlong and Cartmel (1997), while the exemplary case study of this age group is that by Skeggs (1997). Let us start in Kingsport, draw out some of the implications of the Kingsport vignette, and then explore how, if at all, things have changed since 1890 and 1950.

Kingsport University 2005: Scene 5.1

Kellie-Anne Tadman, the youngest secretary in the Sociology Department, is 19 and engaged to be married to Bill Heyer, who is employed by the local council in Kingsport in the parks department in summer, and does snow clearing and gritting in winter. Kellie-Anne was in the same year at school as Chloe Beddows, who is a first-year student. Chloe hasn't seen much of Kellie-Anne since Kellie-Anne left school at 17. When they meet in front of the first-year noticeboard, they are both embarrassed. Chloe can't imagine anyone getting engaged at 19; Kellie-Anne can't imagine why Chloe wants to do a degree.

It is in the years 16–25 that class differences in life experiences show up particularly starkly in contemporary Britain. The lives of Kellie-Anne and Chloe can be paralleled by those of their brothers. Chloe's older brother is a final-year dentistry student at Cardiff, her younger one is doing 'A' levels and hopes to read archaeology at University College London. None of them will marry until they are 28; they will have children in their thirties. Kellie-Anne's older brother Scott left school without any qualifications and has been unemployed or on government schemes since 1996. Her younger brother Wayne did GCSEs and a course in bakery at a further education college; he then joined the army at 18. When he comes home on leave from Catterick he talks vaguely of getting a catering job in Kingsport, taking a stall in the market to sell his 'home-baked' cakes or leaving Kingsport to work on a cruise ship, in a hotel or in London. In these two families, the class differences in contemporary Britain are all too apparent. Kellie-Anne, her fiancé Bill and her brother Scott are all stuck in the working class because they left full-time education before they were 21. They are likely to have low-paid jobs interspersed with unemployment, to live in rented accommodation, to face old age with only the state pension, and to die a decade earlier than peers who become graduates. Chloe and her brothers are destined for careers, mortgages, occupational pensions and longer lives because they have entered higher education.

The biggest division in British society, leading to class-of-adult destination, is based on decisions taken at 16, 18 and 19. People who take 'A' levels or Scottish Highers, or who go into full-time higher education, particularly at elite institutions (Mac an Ghaill 1988; Brown and Scase 1994; Marshall *et al.* 1997), have higher life-time earnings, better pensions, better health and higher status than those who leave education at 16, 18 or 19. Kellie-Anne *could* use her secretarial skills to get a job in an office where she mixes with men in the middle class and marry into that class. In her office work, she will mix with women whose own class of origin, and class of marriage, are higher than hers, and this might raise her ambitions. If she decided to return to education and gain credentials by further full- or part-time study, she could reach a higher class than her current one. However, this is much harder socially and financially than 'staying on' until 18 and 'going on' straightaway. However, her decision to marry Bill, an unskilled labourer, is one that implies a rejection of social mobility by marriage or education. Bill is a typical working-class man who has 'chosen' an unskilled manual job after leaving school at the earliest opportunity: Kellie-Anne's two brothers are equally lacking in academic credentials. Scott is effectively stuck in the unskilled working class or even what is sometimes called the 'underclass'. No credentials and 10 years without a job, only schemes and benefits. He has grown up 'at the margins' (Coffield *et al.* 1986) and become one of the 'working class without work' (Weis 1989). Like the young men attending a course on building (Riseborough 1993b), he has cut himself off from home ownership, health care and will face poverty throughout his adult life.

Wayne's trajectory is more hopeful. Riseborough's (1993a) ethnography of young people doing catering showed that, for some of them, it was a non-academic route to new places and a new life, including a new social class. Fine

(1985) showed how catering, especially being a chef, is a way for working-class Americans to be upwardly mobile and acquire the 'tastes' of a higher social class. If Wayne comes out of the army a good chef, he could get a well-paid post or run his own business (Fine 1996).

The Tadman family has one male in the underclass (Scott) and two who could escape if they make certain choices; however, they seem to lack the fierce ambition needed to rise in Britain without a degree. By not going into higher education, they have made their own futures problematic. Three sets of decisions are crucial: staying on at 16, going on to higher education at 18 and choosing where to undertake higher education. *Any* post-16 education would have helped Scott Tadman; any post-18 course would have helped Kellie-Anne and Wayne. However, while any decision to go into higher education will produce some labour market advantage, British higher education is now a diversified and stratified system. The upper and upper middle classes, especially the intelligentsia or new middle class (Delamont 1989), know where to send their children to maximize their advantage, while other social groups do not.

Brown and Scase (1994) issued a questionnaire to students in three English universities in 1990: at 'Oxbridge', at a university in the 'Home Counties' founded in the 1960s and at 'Inner City', a former polytechnic. They followed up the questionnaire with 120 interviews in 1991 and 1992, and then followed twenty of their student sample into employment. Brown and Scase found that the graduates originally from middle-class homes and those who went to Oxbridge got better jobs and fitted better into the employment they got. The higher education system was reproducing both class and cultural capital inequalities. Choosing to go to 'Inner City' replicated inequalities. The students who 'chose' 'Inner City' were from the poorest and least knowledgeable homes, and they were then handicapped by employer prejudice against degrees gained from 'Inner City'. They found it both harder to find jobs and were less comfortable in the jobs they found than their contemporaries who 'chose' the Oxbridge and Home Counties universities.

A case study of 18-year-olds in Cardiff choosing which higher education institution (HEI) to apply to (Pugsley 1998) shows the importance of the 'choices' and the ways in which class, wealth and poverty, and family familiarity or alienation with higher education, impact on that 'choice'. Pugsley found that the greater the cultural capital of sixth-formers' homes, the more likely their school was to provide detailed help and support to them in choosing their higher education. Sixth-formers in households where no-one before had entered higher education, and nothing was known about it, were at schools where no help was provided. These young people were both attracted to and steered by their teachers to two local HEIs which operated concordats: anyone with two 'A' levels could register for a degree course, anyone with less could start a diploma in higher education. This allowed these young people to enter higher education but to live at home, keep their part-time jobs, maintain existing relationships *and* get credentials. The higher education they 'chose' was, of course, much inferior to that chosen by the middle-class sixth-formers at the elite schools.

Chloe Beddows' two brothers, who have chosen elite, 'Russell Group', universities in Cardiff and University College London, are typical of the young men and women from homes with high levels of knowledge about the education system who are steered into top places. Pugsley (1998: 74) quotes a typical mother from a family at ease with the stratified higher education system: 'My husband is in the university, and his father was a professor at the university . . . we just feel it would be better for her to go to Cambridge'. The contrast with a working-class mother's view of the 'choice' of HEI is striking:

> No we haven't done any of that studying like. We don't understand any of it. This is the first one with all the brains, aren't you? She is the first of my mother's grandchildren to go to university so we are all really proud of her.
>
> (Pugsley 1998: 79)

Similarly, a father, who was explaining to Lesley Pugsley that he found the university application procedures baffling, said: 'I haven't thrown my brains at it . . . I didn't expect any of this, I didn't know that there was this sort of preparatory work which was all piling up' (Pugsley 1998: 80).

A similar differentiation occurs among the young people who remain in education but who choose vocational training rather than academic courses. Riseborough (1993a, b) observed young people doing a BTEC in Catering and Hotel Management and young men on a Youth Training Scheme (YTS) building course. The differences between the 'cream team' and the 'wolf pack' – in their dress and appearance, their leisure interests, their ambitions and their attitudes to attending a higher education college – were as great as those in Pugsley's sample between the elite young women heading for Oxford from the fee-paying school and the baffled working-class sixth-formers at an inner-city comprehensive going to a former polytechnic on a concordat.

Roberts (1993) compared the trajectories of 16- to 19-year-olds in the 1980s with those of a similar age 15 years earlier. Data from Swindon, Kirkcaldy, Liverpool and Sheffield showed that the life chances of young people aged 16–19 depended on social class, race, sex and region (Swindon had jobs, the other three places did not). In Liverpool in 1988–89, 20 per cent of 18- to 19-year-old whites were unemployed, whereas half of the city's African Caribbeans were. For the 'cream team', jobs in catering and hotels offered social and geographical mobility: 'This city is boring really. I don't want to spend the rest of my life in this hole. I'd like to work on board ship for a while' (Ronnie, in Riseborough 1993a: 40). Many of the catering students already had jobs in the industry in their 'own' time; some planned to go on to higher education to study hotel management. In contrast, the 'wolf pack' were active in petty crime and fiddles and had no plans for the future: the YTS course led to unskilled work on (non-existent) building sites (Riseborough 1993b).

I have argued that the biggest division in contemporary society, leading to class-of-adult destination, is a result of the 'choices' made between the ages of 15 and 16 and between 18 and 19. Those who go on to higher education improve every aspect of their life chances; those who try to go into employment are limiting their futures. The consequences of abandoning full-time education at 16 or at 18 are equally severe for males and females. Class is more relevant to this choice than sex or race. Yet to compare 2001 with 1893 or 1951, sex has to be placed alongside class (Bates and Riseborough 1993).

In the 1890s, nearly all 18- to 19-year-olds were in the labour market. Only 1.5 per cent of people went to higher education, mainly young men. Parental money was essential to pay for higher education and to pay for 'apprenticeships' in many white-collar jobs. To start work as a clerk, for example, meant paying a premium to the employer for 'training'. Middle-class parents were much more likely to pay for sons than daughters to learn an occupation. The heroines of *The Odd Women*, training impoverished ladies to take respectable jobs in offices, are modelled on actual feminist campaigners (see Delamont 1989). In the working classes, the gulf between respectable families where young women worked for wages in factories, shops or domestic service, and the underclass where petty crime and prostitution flourished, was considerable. The fictional 'fallen women' and the victims of Jack the Ripper were an 'awful warning' to working-class girls. In the skilled working class, men took pride in earning enough to keep wives and even daughters at home; in the unskilled classes, everyone had to earn what they could. Feminist ideas were novel and revolutionary: women's legal status was one of dependency. The average age of marriage was 26 for women and 28 for men and, in almost all social classes, cohabitation, premarital sex and illegitimate pregnancy doomed a woman to expulsion from family, neighbourhood and even her class. For young men, premarital sexual experience was acceptable if confined to 'bad' women. The double standard was widely adhered to.

By the 1950s, the most striking shift in the lives of young adult women was the reduction in the age of marriage. Young women, especially in the working classes, married younger and started families younger than in 1893 or in 2001. Higher education was still only an option for 4 per cent of young people. It was not until the early 1960s that the expansion of higher education and the introduction of mandatory grants began to make university a possible goal for many 18-year-olds. In the 1950s, the school leaving age was 15 and there were jobs for unqualified 15-year-olds, so most young adults were in paid work. Young women faced marriage bars in many jobs; that is, they had to leave work on marriage. Equal pay was not on the agenda and married women paid a tiny national insurance contribution, and were thus not building up a pension for themselves. The ideology was of early and permanent marriage. Illegitimate births were a disgrace, premarital sex kept a secret from adults. Young adults were segregated in work and outside it to an extent we would today regard as bizarre. And, for young adult men, 2 years had to be spent in the armed forces, thus disrupting their passage to full adulthood and taking them away from their parental homes and families. No such 'rupture' occurred in the lives of young women (see Wilson 1980).

Since the 1950s, the lives of young adults have changed in six ways. First, sex segregation and chaperonage have vanished in most classes and races (except among Islamic, Hindu, Sikh and Cypriot families). Second, the period of economic dependency has been continually extended. The school leaving age was raised to 16 and then, because unemployment benefit was withdrawn from 16- to 18-year-olds, at a time when youth unemployment was high, an autonomous life was made largely impossible for the under-18s. Third, a wide range of consumer goods, mass media products and leisure facilities are marketed aimed at young adults. Fourth, sexual mores have changed, removing much of the stigma from premarital sex, cohabitation and illegitimate births. Fifth, opportunities for higher education and employment are much less sex-segregated than they were in 1890 or 1951, especially for the well-educated. Finally, for young adult women, the idea that they will make a marriage and leave the labour market is inconceivable.

On all these dimensions, the lives of *both* sexes have changed; indeed, the changes in young adulthood for both sexes are so striking that they overshadow any differences between the sexes. Class differences are so stark, especially in the unskilled working class, that they too overshadow differences in life chances between the sexes. However, it is possible that the beliefs, dreams and attitudes of young adult women have changed more compared to those of their great-grandmothers in 1950 than the beliefs, dreams and attitudes of young adult men have changed compared to those of their great-grandfathers. For the young men and women in 'Status Zero', it is certainly the case that they are more socially excluded than equivalent young adults in 1951.

The removal of all benefits from 16- to 18-year-olds has pushed up to 25 per cent of young people into 'Status Zero' (Rees *et al.* 1996). Status Zero young people are not in paid employment, education or on a scheme and, because they are paid no benefits, they vanish from official records. Although modern Britain is a bureaucratic society, which exercises a high degree of surveillance over, and keeps many records on, its population, these young people have 'vanished'. They are not in official work, so they pay no taxes or national insurance and will not appear in labour force records. They are not in any education, so they are not recorded in any institutional statistics. They are not on any training scheme (e.g. YTS), so do not appear on the records of any youth employment agency. Because they are no longer entitled to unemployment benefit, housing benefit or any other welfare payments, they are unknown to the Department of Social Security. Unlikely to be included on the electoral register, these young people have vanished from official records. Some are living with families, being supported, perhaps caring for babies. Some are working in the black economy, some are killing time. The most deprived young adults are homeless, jobless and futureless (Hall, in press). As Rees *et al.* (1996: 231) argue:

> For young men and women such as those who participated in this study, whose family support is weak and who are also cut off from the principal state-provided sources of advice and guidance on employment, it is not surprising that weighing-up the pros and cons of alternative courses of action in the short term should induce a drift into the kinds of casual work . . . and petty crime which we have described. Isolated from effective alternatives, peer networks become a prime source of information and influence.

Even for young people who do not slide into Status Zero, youth unemployment disrupts the passage to adulthood, as Wallace (1987) found in her study on the Isle of Sheppey. Without steady employment, a young person cannot set up home as an autonomous adult. Wallace found that although parenthood and cohabitation might precede proper employment, marriage and the adult status it brings were delayed until the couple had a steady wage.

The major steps of a young adult – leaving home, getting a job, finding a steady sexual partner – are phased very differently for different classes and races. The traditional white middle-class pattern in England is to leave home for university; for the Scots, the working classes and young people from some ethnic minorities (especially for Asian girls), higher education is more likely to be undertaken from 'home' (Barker 1998). For those who do not go to higher education, leaving 'home' is accomplished by marriage or cohabitation (unless the young person has already been effectively turned out by violence, sexual abuse or family breakdown).

In contemporary Britain, unlike the 1890s or even the 1950s, the parental control of both boys and girls is believed to be less. Young adulthood should be a time of increased autonomy. General public disquiet about arranged and enforced marriages among the South Asian population is grounded in this belief in autonomy for young adults. However, the problem pages of popular women's magazines regularly carry letters that report clashes between parents and their young adult children, while the confessional and confrontational daytime TV shows rely on such disagreements for many of their themes. It would be wise to conclude that, for many young adults, parental power and control is still strong in their lives. The following two letters are from a young adult woman and from a mother wishing to control her young adult son and his future wife's sexuality, respectively:

> I'm married and very happy. I'm also five months pregnant but I simply daren't tell my parents. My mum is very strict and she warned me not to get pregnant – she thinks I'm incapable of looking after a baby. My husband's parents are overjoyed and can't see why I haven't told my side of the family, but they don't know what they're like. Please help – I'm terrified they'll guess.
>
> (*Woman*, 16 August 1999)

> My son is 23 and used to be such a loving boy. Now all he thinks about is his girlfriend and we hardly see him. When he told me he'd asked her to marry him, I decided to do a bit of checking up and found out that she's no virgin. In fact, she's had at least four previous boyfriends. I thought my son had a right to know about this but instead of understanding why I did it, he stormed out. Now my husband and I haven't been invited to the wedding.
>
> (*Woman's Own*, 9 August 1999)

In both these cases, the mother of the young adult seems to be unable to accept their autonomy and relate it to their leaving home.

Leaving the parental home and moving to cohabitation or marriage is one major way of marking adulthood. The average age of first marriage has remained much the same in Britain. In 1961, both men and women were, on average, 25 when they married; the average age went down in the late 1960s, but is 28 and 26 respectively in the late 1990s. Although marriage is entered into later, cohabitation has become much more common. In 1981, only 9 per cent of never-married women were cohabiting, whereas in 1997 it was 27 per cent. Three-quarters of people under 30 believe cohabitation is acceptable. The most likely reason for a cohabitation to end is the marriage of the partners (*Social Trends* 1999: 46). The age at which young adults leave their parental home has varied by class over the past 30 years (Leonard 1980). Changes in the costs of housing seem to prolong co-residence with parents. Leaving the parental home has become delayed during the 1990s. In 1998, over half the men aged 20–24 years were living with one or more parent, similar to the figure in 1978.

Leaving home and establishing a household with a partner is caught up with a series of decisions young adults have to make about sexual orientation and the balances of power in their relationships. For the minority of young adults who choose, or discover, a gay or lesbian identity, establishing an adult, autonomous existence involves also 'coming out' to at least some other people. Mac an Ghaill (1999) has outlined the recent research on young men's choice or discovery of their gay identities, and Skeggs (1997) explores the ways in which most young women are 'double distanced' from lesbianism because it is represented 'by both association with pathological class and race contagion and/or as bourgeois individualistic self-expression' (p. 123). As Skeggs argues, 'for women to take up the lesbian identity . . . would mean to disinvest their gains in respectability' (p. 122). These themes are explored more exhaustively in Hawkes (1996); heterosexual young adults are the central focus here.

Most young adults 'choose' a heterosexual identity in adolescence and young adulthood, partly because they have been reared in a culture in which heterosexuality is assumed and taken for granted. Popular culture pulsates with heterosexuality, with such publications as *Loaded* for males and *Red* for young women. West (1999), in summarizing the survey evidence on first heterosexual intercourse, reports that the age at which it occurred fell fastest in the 1950s. Since 1959, the average age for women has fallen from 21 to 17, while for men it has dropped from 20 to 17. However, in the late 1990s, one-fifth of men aged 16–24 are virgins and over one-fifth of women are. The research conducted in London and Manchester by Holland *et al.* (1998) provides a rich and detailed picture of the negotiation of heterosexual identities and practices in contemporary Britain. The authors conclude that, in this sphere, the beliefs and practices of males and females are sharply differentiated, and argue that the young adult male's view of sexual relations is largely unchanged from that of 1951 or 1893. Holland *et al.* (1998: 10) summarize this position as follows:

> Men's access to positive conceptions of an active, pleasure-seeking, embodied, masculine sexuality, put particular pressures on them to become 'real men' . . . [which] implies the exercise of power over women, whether or not this is recognised, acknowledged, or desired by an individual man . . . young men have considerable power that is not available to young women.

Holland *et al.* argue that, in contrast, young women live feminine identities, 'but in relation to a male audience – measuring themselves through the gaze of the "male-in-the head"' (p. 11). Although a decade has passed since they collected their data, there is *no* sign that this has changed and there is every indication that the power of the male extends beyond sexualities (Connell 1995).

The problem pages of the women's magazines suggest that young couples may have considerable differences of opinion over male power and female autonomy. For example, *Woman's Own* (16 August 1999) – who announce 'Our guarantee: all our letters are genuine' – carried one example about careers:

> I've known my boyfriend for three years, and we're planning to get married next year. The only thing is I'm starting to have doubts. He was offered a job at the other end of the country and took it for granted that I wouldn't mind leaving my job to go with him. In fact, when I pointed out that I had a career to think of too, he laughed his head off. I've been promoted three times and really love my job. I would be prepared to move for him, I just don't like his attitude.

Note that the young woman is not stating a fixed belief that she should not leave her job and move with her fiancé. She is prepared to do so. However, she wants a negotiation, a recognition of her working life, rather than an assumption of her submission. The legitimacy of the young woman's views is endorsed by the agony aunt who said the man's attitude 'stinks' and advised the woman to 'stand up to him now'.

On sexual behaviour, an engaged woman's letter was published in the same magazine on 9 August 1999:

> We're getting married in the autumn and can't agree on our hen and stag nights. If he's going to go out, get drunk and see a stripper, he can hardly disagree if I do the same. But he says stag nights are different, and that it's only a bit of fun. He hates the idea of me dancing on a table with a naked guy.

The answer again stressed autonomy and equality: either you both have a stripper or neither does. In these two letters, young women are arguing for some measure of equality, which is endorsed by the agony aunts (or, at least, the right to be treated as a partner in a negotiation). Young women expressing similar desires for equality in 1951 and 1890 were firmly told by magazine writers that their duty was to obey, sacrifice and submit.

One subset of young adult women are not able to be equal, either to young males or other women – that is, the minority who enter young adulthood already as mothers. In 1996, there were 44,700 babies born to young women aged 15–19. Teenage births account for 20 per cent of all illegitimate births, and 80–90 per cent of all teenage births take place outside marriage (McRae 1999). The mothers of babies and small children, whether married or single, spend young adulthood in poverty and frequently in social housing. Allen and Dowling (1999) interviewed 84 women in London, Leeds and Solihull who had had a baby in 1995 when aged 16–19. Only 15 per cent of them were in employment, 80 per cent were on income support and half were no longer in a relationship with the father. One-third were in local authority housing and a further third on waiting lists. Many were living alone with their young child and were lonely. The vibrant world of leisure and flamboyant lifestyles was closed to them.

Leisure, lifestyles, life choices

Furlong and Cartmel (1997) summarize the research in this area. Leisure activities among young people are gendered, differentiated by class and by status. Students, for example, have more active leisure pursuits than the unemployed, even though the latter have more 'spare' time. There is far more research on young men's leisure than on that of young women. Canaan (1996) explored the ways in which unemployed and marginally employed young men 'do nothing' as a leisure activity, partly because their lack of money prevents them going to soccer games, pubs or clubs. Furlong and Cartmel (1997: 59) conclude that 'those who spend time out of work tend to lead narrow and unfulfilling leisure lifestyles'.

Young men are more likely to play and to watch sport than young women: the middle classes are more likely to go to theatres and cinemas than the working class. Location also makes a difference. Young adults in cities like Manchester (Redhead 1993) and Newcastle (Bennett 1999) have more opportunities to choose between different types of club with different types of music than a person in a rural area or a small town. Young adults from ethnic minorities may be unable to participate in activities because of fear of racial violence; young women may be careful to avoid 'danger'.

Social scientists have focused most on urban working-class men, especially those active in 'youth cultures'. There are few studies on young adults who go to evening classes, sing in church choirs, belong to camera clubs or run brownie packs. This is partly because the sociologies of youth, consumption and culture all have an anti-intellectual bias. Fans of The Prodigy are a more appropriate topic than fans of Sir Simon Rattle or the Royal Shakespeare Company; Manchester City supporters are more 'interesting' than lovers of Picasso's blue period or Rachel Whiteread's sculptures. The sociology of culture is actually the study of low-brow, anti-intellectual popular culture – the equivalent of the hooligan in the school (Delamont 2000a). Research on young adults in an audience at Wexford for the opera smacks of elitism in the way that a project on body-builders does not. A project on real tennis or squash would be less acceptable than one on greyhound racing.

The emphasis in the sociology of leisure and lifestyles, especially in adolescence and young adulthood, on the anti-intellectual and the lowbrow, does not mean that the studies are poorly done. The research on anti-intellectual, lowbrow culture and consumption is usually of a high standard. For example, King (1997) studied a group of Manchester United fans, men aged 19–48 years, whose masculinity was closely tied to dress (expensive designer label casual clothing), drinking, singing and fighting as 'Reds'. Their response to new all-seater stadia were mixed. Pride in the quality of the facilities at Old Trafford, but anger at the destruction of a working-class, physical solidarity and style (standing, swaying, singing), characterized their response. The problem is that the lives of young men who revere Part or Neilson are not studied at all. A project on the people who stand, sway and applaud at the Proms is needed to counterbalance the work of King, Redhead and Bennett. More studies of young adult women are also required to counterbalance the work on young men, studies that do not simply focus on 'youth culture'.

Verdict

Have the lives of the young adult women changed while those of young men have not? Certainly the lives of men and women in all social classes are very different from those in 1893, because of increased education, mobility, widening leisure activities and a reduction in sex segregation. Young women have opportunities for higher education and careers that were undreamt of in 1893. Compared to 1951, however, the changes have not been so dramatic. Rather, the inequalities of class and the hegemony of the heterosexual male gaze were apparent in 1951, and the evidence suggests that there has been little change over the past 50 years. A young adult woman who has a degree and is single has very different life chances from one who has no credentials and a young child. These class differences have not narrowed since 1951 and, at the present time, are more divisive than differences between the sexes. If we compare young adult men and women within each social class, their life chances, attitudes and behaviour are different from those of equivalent young adults in 1951 in superficial ways (no National Service, less stigma on unmarried mothers), but there is not enough evidence to claim that one sex *has* changed while the other has not. There are some hints and a few studies that suggest this, but the research base is not strong enough to confirm it.

Further reading

Bates, I. and Riseborough, G. (eds) (1993) *Youth and Inequality*. Buckingham: Open University Press.
Hall, T. (in press) *No Place Like Home*. London: Pluto Press.
Skeggs, B. (1997) *Formation of Class and Gender*. London: Sage.

Part **three**
ADULTHOOD: *the* RECEIVED WISDOM QUERIED

In Part three, four chapters examine the central issue, is it *true* that women have changed and men haven't? There are four sociologically distinguishable spheres: (i) the body (where the stigmatized, sick or deviant identity crystallizes the issue of changes in gender roles); (ii) consumption/locality (where the place of residence as experienced by men and women *can* be mediated by consumption and non-consumption); (iii) work (where new forms of post-industrial and post-fordist labour may reinforce new, or old, gender roles); (iv) the home (where the myth locates the new woman and the old man).

The biggest shift in sociology over the past 20 years has been from a focus on the public (paid work, political behaviour, street crime, trade union-ism, the stigma of membership of outcast groups, ethnic relations, class) to the private (housework, caring, domestic violence, food, child abuse, the body, identity). Traditionally, men have gained a substantial portion of their iden-tity from work: a man was a carpenter, a soldier, a fisherman, a docker, a miner, a doctor, a solicitor, a playwright. Women's identity came from being a wife (a carpenter's wife, a soldier's wife, a fisherman's wife, a docker's wife, a miner's wife, a doctor's wife, a solicitor's wife, a playwright's wife) and a mother, and from being sexually respectable (i.e. *not* a slut, a slapper, a tart, a prostitute) and running a tidy house (passing the Daz doorstep challenge).

Such occupational and marital identities were related to class identities and often to localities such as the miners and miners' wives in the mining community (Dicks 2000). The anxieties about de-industrialization, de-skilling, post-traditionalism and globalization expressed by social scientists and mass media pundits are, essentially, speculations about how *men* are to cope with-out those certainties of occupation, class and locality. Much less has been written about how women are to cope without the certainties of occupation, class and locality in their own right, or in the lives of the men in their families. The chapters in this part of the book focus on these issues and, importantly, reflecting that displacement of work and marriage, those themes come *after* the new preoccupations on bodies and consumption patterns.

As a way of opening up our thinking on what women's lives are like in an era of de-industrialization and globalization, it is informative to study the mass readership of women's magazines. The problem pages of the women's magazines offer an intriguing picture of contemporary life. They used to send out leaflets, but now advertise telephone helplines. The topics that they promote give an interesting summary of what common problems face adult women in Britain: we can assume that the topics offered serve a market need (i.e. people phone them). Helplines make a profit for their owners: unpopular topics would not survive. The helplines provided by four mass-market magazines (*Chat, Woman, Woman's Own* and *Woman's Realm*) offer the following:

Woman's Realm
- Ways out of the blues
- Creating confidence
- Slimming tricks
- Banishing panic and worry
- Shaking off loneliness
- Refreshing a marriage

Woman
- I'm always anxious
- I feel so lonely
- My partner hits me
- Should I get divorced?
- Why am I so depressed?
- I can't have an orgasm
- I'm pregnant – it wasn't planned
- We're splitting up
- I'm so jealous
- I don't have any confidence
- How can I improve my sex life?
- He's having an affair

Woman's Own
- Make new friends
- Putting back the romance
- Boost your confidence
- Boost your sex drive
- Love after divorce
- Can you stay together after an affair?
- How to cope with depression
- Problems with teenagers
- What a man likes best in bed
- Jealousy
- Stand up for yourself
- Coping with splitting up

Chat
- Learn to orgasm
- No more panic attacks
- Worried about oral sex?
- What's good in bed?

- Finding Mr Right
- Beating bowel problems

There are several common themes here and they paint a bleak picture. The reader of a woman's magazine faces many problems. She is psychologically troubled (anxious, suffering panic attacks, depressed, lacking self-confidence and unable to stand up for herself). She has an inadequate social life (lonely, seeking Mr Right). Her relationship is problematic (she is jealous, her marriage needs refreshing, he hits her, there are affairs or divorces). Her sex life needs repair, she is pregnant, believes she needs to slim or has bowel problems. Noticeably, none of these lines deals with work or employment, or practical issues such as benefits, housing, legal rights, educational topics or dealing with the National Health Service. They address body image and health, family life and psychological well-being. In the following four chapters, the research evidence on these problems is scrutinized.

6 Stigma, deviance, bodies *and* identity

> The person was Miss Eade, her old acquaintance of the shop. But the girl no longer dressed as in those days; cheap finery of the 'loudest' description arrayed her form, and it needed little scrutiny to perceive that her thin cheeks were artificially reddened.
>
> (Gissing 1893/1980: 297)

> Women are trammelled by their clothes: to be able to get rid of them, and to move about with free and brave exertion of all the body, must tend to every kind of health, physical, mental and moral.
>
> (Gissing 1893/1980: 256)

In these two quotes from *The Odd Women*, issues of self-presentation, clothing and bodies are presented as central to wider issues of work, freedom and morality in 1893. Miss Eade has left behind the drudgery of shopwork and become a prostitute, soliciting on Victoria Station. Her clothes, and the rouge on her cheeks, betray her moral descent. In the second quote, Everard, who is the nearest thing the novel has to a hero, bemoans the restrictive rules of polite society which prevent ladies learning to swim. He argues that the freedom from restrictive clothing and healthy exercise would bring many benefits. In contemporary Britain, street prostitutes still have distinctive dress styles, although make-up and swimming are no longer considered impossible for most women. In this chapter, sociological analyses of such bodily issues as dress, make-up and swimming are explored.

This chapter explores the evidence on the roles of men and women in contemporary Britain in terms of the body, focusing on 'perfect' and 'stigmatized' bodies, 'straight' or 'deviant' identities, and dealing with current debates from the sociologies of crime and health and illness. The focus is on men and women over 25, comparing their embodiment; that is, a focus on stigma, deviance and the body in the lives of men and women in 2001 compared to men and women in the 1890s and the early 1950s. The changes, if any, in the patterns of gender and illness are explored. The themes of this chapter are hard to use as a basis for comparisons with 1890 or 1950 because data on stigma, deviance, bodies and health are difficult to obtain and more difficult to compare. In a modern confessional culture (Atkinson and Silverman 1997), we can learn a good deal about how people regard their bodies, about deviant behaviour, about experience of illness and what they feel is stigmatizing. Such data are simply not retrievable from previous eras.

In 1890, both males and females were probably dissatisfied with their bodies, much as they are today, although the 'ideal' appearance was different. For example, a pale skin, which indicated a lady-like indoor leisured life, was desirable in the 1890s, unlike the tanned skin preferred today despite health advice on skin cancer. Beards and moustaches were more common; no doubt men unable to grow them felt 'incomplete'. Behaviours seen as deviant were different, as was the range of crimes punishable in court. Today many men and women become involved with the police and the courts because of motoring offences, for which there is no 1890 equivalent. Patterns of health and illness have changed, as has the availability of health care. Many women died in childbirth and both sexes died of infectious diseases, including cholera, scarlet fever and tuberculosis, that are now rare or curable. Yet there are continuities. One of the sad spinster daughters of Dr Madden is an alcoholic: a secret shame. There was drug addiction, burglary, rape and hooliganism.

Similarly, there are changes and continuities between 2001 and 1951. Both sexes were dissatisfied with their bodies, although the desired shapes had changed from 1893 and are different again now. By 1951, Britain had the National Health Service, which made health care available to the working classes, especially women. Infectious diseases were in decline, as was death in childbirth. Many 'crimes' were the same in 1951 as they had been in 1893, including suicide and male homosexuality, and the death penalty was in use. Looking back from 2001, one form of crime and deviance, buying petrol, food or clothes without the proper ration books, in which many otherwise respectable people were engaged between 1940 and the early 1950s, has been forgotten. Many men alive in 1951 had health problems (mental or physical) stemming from war service in 1914–18 or 1939–45: these are rarer today and were rarer in 1890.

One of the biggest changes between 1893 and 1951 compared to 2001 is the amount of leisure time that is available to the middle and working classes, especially to men, the variety of activities available and the distances travelled for leisure. However, leisure activities, especially sporting ones, are strongly gendered in 2001, as strongly gendered as they were in 1893 and 1951. Let us start among the Kingsport students and staff:

Kingsport University 2005: Scene 6.1

Chloe Beddows, Emma Tuke and Grace Pinker, all first years, are at their capoeira class in the small gym at the union. Capoeira is a Brazilian martial art/dance form which has become a fitness/exercise craze in Kingsport following aerobics and line dancing. Emma is assistant secretary of the union's capoeira society and is quite good: her friends are beginners, who've been swept up by Emma and brought along to try it. After class they have plans to meet David Shirley and some of his friends, who are doing weight training elsewhere in the union weights room.

Elsewhere in the city Dr Ross Crossfield is playing squash at a leisure centre, Bill Heyer is training with his pub soccer team, and Reg Aythorne, a technician in Engineering, is digging his allotment.

This capoeira class/session focuses our attention on 'those doggedly fleshy, troubling matters of female embodiment' as Hughes and Witz (1997: 56) characterize them. The leotard lesson (Delamont 1998) discussed in Chapter 4 displays discourse about four ways in which female students' adolescent bodies were disciplined in their secondary school years which are embodiments of the four dimensions outlined by Frank (1990, 1991). In their late teens and twenties, such bodily disciplines are left to young women themselves, and only involve team games and gymnastics for a tiny minority. Voluntary exercise such as aerobics is more common. That equivalent men should be weight training fits the gendered nature of body maintenance in modern Britain (Monaghan 1999).

Three other men are engaged in leisure activities, common for their age and class: squash, soccer and gardening. Their wives and fiancée are not involved in any leisure activities. In adulthood, leisure is strongly gendered and closely related to issues of stigma, deviance and identity, which are central to who we are and whether we feel 'entire and whole and perfect'. Research on leisure (e.g. Deem 1986; Deem and Gilroy 1998) shows repeatedly that women with households have little 'leisure' unless it is combined with child care or taken with partners, and such leisure as they do have is not usually sporting. As this chapter unfolds, the role of weight training, squash, soccer and gardening in men's lives will become clearer.

Theoretical background: The contested body

Frank (1990, 1991) argued that sociology had fallen behind other spheres of academic discourse because sociologists were neglecting to afford 'centrality to the body'. Frank then divided the literature into substantive categories, those of the *talking* bodies, *disciplined* bodies, *sexual* bodies and *medicalized* bodies. Each is an ideal type, based on responses to four issues – other-relatedness, self-relatedness, desire and control – all of which derive from the theories of Foucault (1979).

Frank (1991) argued that the term the 'disciplined body' describes one style of body use and body-to-object relatedness along these four dimensions. The bodies of people skilled at capoeira or committed to weight training are disciplined bodies. Frank himself illustrates the disciplined body with examples from military drill, holy anorexia in medieval mystics and professional dance. For many men in manual jobs, their work demanded, and produced, disciplined bodies. As traditional agricultural and industrial employment has vanished, so too have the body types once associated with them. Many men and women in modern Britain see their bodies as a source of stigma: they believe that their bodies are inferior, that they fall short of some ideal. Take the letter printed in *Woman* (16 August 1999):

> I can't stand the way I look. My teeth are crooked, I have very small breasts, stretchmarks on my tummy, varicose veins on my legs and

bunions on my big toes. I've taken advice for all these things but I can't afford surgery or dentistry and there's no other answer. My husband says he loves me and that he's also not perfect, but I long to feel normal and confident. I feel guilty because I'm a Christian and I know that I shouldn't be so selfish.

This woman's letter could have been written at any time in the past 50 years. Indeed, it could have been published in *Stigma*, the classic text written by Erving Goffman in 1963. No-one has bettered his analysis yet. For this book, there is no need to challenge Goffman's analysis, only to explore what aspects of identity are stigmatizing for women and men in contemporary Britain.

For many women in Britain, body size is the biggest stigma: fear of being seen, or seeing oneself, as fat is an ever-present terror. There is an industry targeted at these women: magazines, diet books, slimming clubs, special foods and fiercesome corsets (although these are less common than they were 30 years ago). The 'ideal' body size has got smaller since the 1950s; the fatter woman is increasingly stigmatized and more of the population are 'overweight'. Discrimination against fat women is common, in employment in particular. Tyler and Abbott (1998) studied the recruitment and training of flight attendants by two airlines and their subsequent supervision in employment. Part of the routine grooming checks on women were 'weight checks' to ensure they were maintaining a strict height-to-weight ratio. Male flight attendants were not weighed. There was even a belief among the women that the uniforms were deliberately labelled with the 'wrong size', so that a size 8 uniform would have '10' in it to scare women into staying slim when their airline clothing felt 'tight'. For some women, pregnancy 'solves' certain problems around bodies: the edges of the self are blurred and some of the 'requirements' of slimness, beauty and style can be ignored (Bailey 1999). However, few women take part in sport to reduce weight, because a muscled physique is also seen as 'unfeminine' (Deem and Gilroy 1998). Men are less self-conscious about body size and are less subject to hegemonic gaze. However, some fat men also join clubs, adopt diets and attempt to lose weight, and feel stigmatized because of their weight.

Although sociologists have focused on the body in the past decade, many other things impact on our sense of identity and are sources of stigma. For example, for married couples, being unable to have children when they are wanted is stigmatizing (Humphrey 1969; Owens 1982). (Being childless by choice is being child-free, and is stigmatizing in a different way.) Owens's (1982) work on men in subfertile couples found that they felt they had failed both as men *and* as husbands. That is, men believed that a good husband fathered children so his wife could experience motherhood, a state they understood to be highly desirable for women. Some of Owens's respondents said that if they could not father children, they would expect their wives to divorce them and remarry to achieve motherhood. Macintyre's (1977) seminal study in Aberdeen, which explored the reproductive ideologies (Busfield 1974) of young women, general practitioners and gynaecologists, should alert us to the fact that not *all* married women do wish to be mothers;

nevertheless, for many women, being childless is a stigma. Becoming a mother is an important part of attaining adult identity.

A series of studies of women's passage to motherhood (e.g. Oakley 1979; Phoenix *et al.* 1991; Bailey 1999) has confirmed the persistence of what Busfield (1974) called the 'dominant British reproductive ideology'. There is a powerful set of beliefs that motherhood is fulfilling for women, and that couples who do not become parents are 'selfish'. Bailey (1999) interviewed 30 women in Bristol about to have their first baby. They were all white and their average age was 32. These women all reported a raising of their status because of the pregnancy: they saw themselves as being 'responsible', brought up to the level of other adults, and 'slotted in to what a woman can do' (p. 341). The stigma attached to the involuntarily childless or to being child-free is considerable, even though one in five women born in 1961 will remain childless or child-free (ONS 1998).

One change from Britain 30 or 40 years ago is the decline in the 'shame' attached to illegitimacy, both for the mother and the child. One-third of live births in 1997 were 'illegitimate', but four-fifths of these were registered by both parents and three-quarters of them by cohabiting parents (*Social Trends* 1999: 50). For individual women, illegitimacy may still be stigmatizing, but in general it is an acceptable 'choice' for a woman over 20 and only frowned on in a young teenager, a 'girl' of 12–16. For married women and women over 18 in 'secure' cohabitations, becoming a mother is a source of securing an adult identity. Removing the stigma of childlessness and taking on the identity of mother does, however, bring women up against the health service and, for many, introduces a series of hardships (Graham 1993).

Health and illness

British sociology is particularly strong in the area of health and illness, where gender is an important topic. There are differences in life expectancy, causes of illness and death, and uses made of the health services between men and women. Women live longer and use the health services more. Acheson (1998) summarizes the literature on health inequalities in Britain and Annandale and Hunt (2000) focus on gender inequalities specifically. Racial inequalities in health are explored in Acheson (1998).

Life expectancy has risen in Britain since the 1890s, but for many people the later years of life are clouded by chronic illness or disability. Class differences in health are large and they widened in the 1970s and 1980s. These class differences are much starker for men. Acheson (1998: 14) estimated that 17,000 unskilled men aged 20–64 die every year when men in other social classes live beyond retirement age. These premature and unnecessary deaths are due to heart disease, accidents, suicide, lung cancer, other cancers, other respiratory disease and strokes, all of which kill more men in the unskilled class than in the higher social classes. Some of this is self-inflicted (smoking is practised more widely among the working classes, whose diets lack fresh fruit and fibre), but some is due to inequalities in, for example, the stress and danger of the workplace.

The overall gender differences in health cannot, however, be seen as 'new'. Poverty and a poor diet are particular problems for working-class pregnant women, mothers of young children and elderly women without any income but the state pension. This was true in 1893, 1951 and 1969. Working-class boys and young men are likely to die in accidents or as a direct result of violence; youths abuse their bodies with drink, drugs and tobacco, and are more vulnerable to suicide than elderly men, especially widowers (the rates are four times higher in social class five than in class one among men under 44). These are long-standing patterns. Health inequalities are strongly linked to class and poverty, and gender differences in health are striking. Graham (1993) presents the evidence on hardship and women's health, with data on women from several different ethnic groups.

Annandale (1998) argues that male life expectancy may be starting to rise towards that of women, perhaps because of women's increased smoking and the decline of dangerous industrial work (e.g. mining) for men. Some of the old male-dominated industries also led to early deaths in men, for example pneumoconiosis in miners. Annandale points out that changes in female smoking and male employment will feed into life expectancy over the next 50 years. There have also been claims that women live longer *because* they consult doctors more; that is, they may benefit because they seek help and treatment while diseases are 'treatable', whereas men delay consultation until diseases are far advanced.

There is no doubt that women use the health services more; however, it is unclear whether this is because they *are* more unwell or are more willing to admit to sickness. Data on consulting the family doctor, on hospital admissions and from self-report surveys, all show women as being more sick. Certainly women are 29 per cent more likely to be admitted to hospital for mental illnesses and are more likely to consult general practitioners for anxiety, depression and other 'mental' problems, such as feeling 'tired all the time' and 'nerves'. The consensus among medical sociologists is that women have more illness than men, although it is not clear why. When men and women with 'the same' symptoms are compared, men are more likely to rate themselves as 'seriously ill', apparently reinforcing the old joke that 'his' cold is flu and 'hers' is a 'mere sniffle'. He must retire to bed, she can continue with her full workload (Macintyre 1993). Although this sounds like a plot from a bad TV sitcom, there is research evidence to reinforce it (Annandale 1998).

Women suffer more mental illness than men and are more likely to perform their everyday tasks while taking prescribed mood-changing medication (Gabe and Thorogood 1986). There is also a different relationship between marriage and health if we compare men and women. Men are healthier if married, whereas women are healthier if they are single. This may be a class inequality, however, because the 'never married' are disproportionately the best-qualified and highest earning women, and the worst-qualified and most unemployed men. Some forms of illness and disability are much more stigmatizing than others. Mental illness, drug addiction, HIV/AIDS, epilepsy and intestinal surgery that leaves the sufferer managing a colestomy bag can cause people to lose their jobs, be evicted, be abandoned by their families and be refused entry to leisure facilities. People with these conditions may hide them from others. Gender differences interact with the effects of these conditions in complex ways. Agoraphobia – that is, a fear of crowds that forces sufferers to cower indoors because they have disabling panic attacks in public spaces – is much more stigmatizing for men than women, because it is more socially acceptable for a woman to stay indoors, not to take paid employment, not to go to pubs or clubs, not to be playing golf or be on the local council.

There also is a feminist literature on how the medical professions (especially male doctors) treat women patients. The tone of this literature is captured by the title of Helen Roberts's (1985) book, *The Patient Patients*. Feminists have argued that doctors are trained to treat women in stereotyped ways, ignoring their knowledge of their own bodies and enforcing male medical models. This strand of argument is focused on mental illness, on childbirth, on gynaecology and on interactions with small children. The research on women seeking contraception, abortion and sterilizations has argued that women receive very different advice if they are unmarried as opposed to being married, and that women of different classes and races may be treated in contrasting ways. However, most of these studies were based on retrospective interviews, rather than on direct observation, were small-scale in nature and rarely matched with studies of male patients. The papers collected by Annandale and Hunt (2000), which argue for researchers to focus on gender differences in health and illness rather than just on women, suggest a way forward. Currently, gender and health is an area affected by de-industrialization and changing labour markets. However, as with many other aspects of British life, class differences are as marked as gender differences. The health of two doctors who are male and female is more similar than either's similarity to an unskilled worker of the same sex.

Stigma, deviance and crime

There is an overlap between stigma, deviance and crime. Stigmatized individuals are likely to be victims; people labelled 'deviant' are more frequently attacked. An example of this is being gay or lesbian: while many gay and lesbian people reject the very idea that they *are* deviant or bear a stigma, there are those who feel deviant and who feel stigmatized. Whether 'out and proud' or 'closeted and ashamed', however, gay and lesbian people are vulnerable to attack – are vulnerable to be victims of crime and abuse.

Richardson and May (1999) report a national survey of 4000 lesbians and gay men. A third of the gay men and a quarter of the lesbians surveyed reported that they had been attacked by a stranger in a public place at least once in the past 5 years. The rates of attack were higher for African Caribbean, Asian and disabled people in the sample. Gay men are more likely to report attacks near gay clubs and pubs or cruising and cottaging sites, lesbians in the 'ordinary' streets. Most of the accounts of violence on gay men say the attackers were young men. David Copeland, who put a bomb in a gay pub in Soho in 1999, was an extreme example of a young man who felt free to kill gay men. Two things are striking about this pattern. First, there is a similarity with attacks on African Caribbean and Asian people, like Stephen Lawrence (Cathcart 2000), Ricky Freel and others. Copeland had also placed bombs in Brixton to kill African Caribbeans and in Brick Lane to kill South Asians. Both racial minorities and gays and lesbians suffer public violence (for further discussion, see Mac an Ghaill 1999). Second, lesbians suffer public violence in the street, whereas most women are at risk of abuse in their homes (see Chapter 8).

There are three aspects of deviance and crime which receive attention here: gender differences in victimhood and in fear of crime; gender differences in criminal activity, such as whether the stresses experienced by men are leading/driving them into deviance (such as drug addiction) and crime (vandalism, violence, rape); and whether women's changing roles include more criminal activity. The third aspect reflects how far the changing roles of men and women are influencing their roles in law enforcement. There are several good secondary sources on gender and criminology (e.g. Walklate 1995; Heidensohn 1996). In this section, I deal only with a few issues of crime in public places and deviant behaviour and identities. (Domestic violence and other aspects of crime 'at home' are dealt with in Chapter 8.)

The first way in which crime and deviance are related to identity is via the motor car. Driving is the main 'cause' of criminality and 'deviance' in the UK. In 1982, for example, the courts in England and Wales (Scotland and N. Ireland have their own legal systems, and separate crime figures are kept and published) found two million adults guilty of something (some of whom will have been tried more than once). However, over one million of these offenders had broken a motoring law. Although many more automatic penalties were introduced in 1986 without court appearances, still 2,163,000 motoring offences were taken to court in the UK (*Social Trends* 1999: 189). Although Britain's motorists commit a lot of offences (speeding, driving while drunk, driving while uninsured, parking illegally, etc.), they are rarely *labelled* 'criminals' or 'deviants'. Killing an 'innocent' person, especially when drink-driving or driving a stolen or uninsured car, is seen as bad or even criminal, but in general those found guilty of motoring offences are not branded criminals. An anti-road protester or a person who refuses to drive based on principle rather than poverty *is* seen as deviant, a person who breaks the speed limit is not. Breaking the speed limit is not seen as 'serious', even though it puts lives (especially children's lives) at risk.

In modern Britain, the people generally regarded as 'real' criminals are those cautioned for, or found guilty of, indictable offences such as burglary or stealing a car. Such people are overwhelmingly male. In 1982, 89 per cent of those found guilty in a court in England and Wales were male; in 1997, 83 per cent of those found guilty or cautioned in England and Wales were men (*Social Trends* 1999: 156). Most of these males are young – the 'typical' criminal is 18 – and most crime is against property. Men are more involved in all types of crime than women, from petty vandalism to murder, and including white-collar crime as well as 'manual' offences like theft. Although women are increasingly being prosecuted and imprisoned, their offences are frequently 'trivial' in that their thefts are small, their violence aimed at only one person, their behaviour self-damaging. The offences women do commit are rarely glamorous or sensational. Shoplifting, prostitution and handling stolen goods do not have the appeal of the Great Train Robbers or the Kray gang or the terrorizing power of Fred West, the Yorkshire Ripper or Hannibal Lector.

Wincup's (1997) study of women on bail reveals criminals driven by poverty and hardship, often compounded by drug addiction, quite unlike the male criminals studied by Hobbs (1988) or Gill (2000). Criminology has been sexist in its focus, with most attention paid to male criminals (Gelsthorpe and Morris 1990; Newburn and Stanko 1994). As far as the sex of criminals is concerned, there has been no change since 1893 or 1951 (Newburn and Stanko 1994). Men are more often criminals than women, their crimes are bigger (whether physical theft or fraud), they are much more violent and their crimes are much more congruent with 'core' masculine values. Despite occasional moral panics in the media, there is no evidence that women are becoming more violent or more criminal.

When we turn to victims, the poorest and most deprived are the most likely to be victims. Class is more salient than gender. The groups in Britain most likely to be murdered are infants under one followed by males aged 16–29. Those living in inner cities, especially in council houses or other social housing, and those who are unemployed, single parents or have low incomes are more vulnerable to burglary. Those who live in detached owner-occupied housing with good salaries are the least likely to be burgled, especially in suburban or rural areas. However, the facts are not related to the level of fear of crime. People in affluent areas fear burglary and spend money on private policing, alarms, floodlights and other precautions. Women and the elderly fear violence, especially violence on the streets from strangers.

One of the paradoxes of contemporary Britain is that the section of the population most likely to suffer a violent attack is men aged 16–25, who spend the most time 'out' – in pubs, clubs, sports grounds and the streets – while the section of the population least likely to be attacked in public places (women over 65) spend the least time 'out'. Of course, the young men are also likely to be the attackers as well as the victims. That is, men between 16 and 25 are the most likely to be injured in public places by other men aged 16–25. A young man who stays at home or says he is scared to go out is seen as a deviant weirdo. In contrast, a woman of 75 who says she is too frightened to walk about the streets at midnight is seen as a rational helpless victim of a wicked society, and no-one would believe she was going to attack anyone if she went out. A man of 20 leaving a pub will fear another man like himself, while an elderly woman coming home from the laundrette after 10 at night would not 'fear' attack by another elderly woman. In the least fearful but most vulnerable group, the 'victims' and the 'attackers' are in the same age and sex category, while those who are most frightened fear young men often of another class and race. Part of the moral panic about men, especially young working-class men, is that they are *increasingly* turning to crime, violence and drugs. Such fears are perennial, as Pearson (1983) shows vividly. The nation that hanged Derek Bentley in the early 1950s (a learning-disabled simpleton who was not carrying the gun which was used to kill a policeman) was just as troubled by fear of working-class boys being criminally violent as the readers of the *Daily Mail* are today. We are all much more likely to be killed by a driver speeding than a violent 'thug' and that driver may be a middle-aged man in a respectable profession, not a young 'hooligan'.

There have been some changes in 'public' violence. The Internet is a new space where women can be abused and terrified (Gillespie 2000). Women can be cyberstalked in cyber space. Pornography and prostitution now occur on websites and via phone lines as well as being accessed in 'real' places (see Radford *et al.* 2000). There is also violence aimed at ethnic minorities and gays and lesbians in these new virtual worlds. The opposite of the 'criminal' is the law enforcer. Here, issues of race, sex and sexual orientation, which are fundamental to identity, are particularly relevant. For most ethnic minorities, entering the police force would be stigmatizing: their same-race peers are likely to avoid them *and* they may be racially abused by their 'colleagues' in the force. Law enforcement is still predominantly in the hands of white men. In 1998, only 16 per cent of police officers in England and Wales were women and only 2 per cent were from the black or Asian ethnic minorities. The police force of 124,798 people was not representative of the population it served, and the studies of 'canteen culture' in the force report endemic hostility to women, gays, lesbians and members of ethnic minorities (see Fielding 1994). Studies of prison officers reveal a similar set of values. It is easier for all three categories (women, gays and lesbians, ethnic minorities) to become members of the other branches of law enforcement – the probation service, and the lower ranks of the legal profession (i.e. solicitors not judges) – and retain their identities in their own communities. That is, it is less stigmatizing for a young African Caribbean male to become a solicitor than a policeman.

However, this does not mean that the occupations enforcing the law are themselves free of homophobia, sexism and racism. Women who become lawyers are frequently unable to work in spheres other than family law and child care. The legal professions, including the Crown Prosecution Service, have been accused of institutional racism. However, no study on racism, sexism or homophobia in the legal professions or probation service has reported harassment as pronounced as that in the police and the prison service.

Conclusions

A frequent argument about the contemporary world is that individuals have multiple identities, grounded in their bodies, their consumption patterns and the presence or absence of various stigmas. The evidence on all matters pertaining to the body, such as health and illness, physical activity and leisure, shows that the basic ascribed categories of class, race and sex are more important factors in producing the unstigmatized body than anything in the power of the individual. Successful athletes with 'perfect' bodies are harassed by the police if they are black; even middle-class white women believe they are not seen as fully adult until they are mothers. It is possible that more people believe that they are individually responsible for their health, bodily features and involvement with crime as victim or perpetrator than did so 50 or 100 years ago. In one way, women are more able to control their health than they were in 1893 or 1951: childbearing can be controlled. Many women in 1893 faced health problems because of multiple childbearing; today, effective contraception and legal abortion mean that most women can be healthier because they can reduce the number and frequency of pregnancies. However, this 'empowerment' is counterbalanced by the obsession with body weight and the 'guilt' about lacking a perfect body, as expressed in the letter reproduced on pp. 63–4.

Verdict

Have women changed their outlook on issues of stigma, bodies, deviance and identity while men have not? The evidence on these issues from 1893 to 1951 is not robust enough to allow us to reach a firm conclusion, but I suspect not. The changes in health, crime, deviance and stigma between 1893 and 2001 have been considerable for both sexes. Class differences remain strong and racial inequalities are deep and wide. However, there is no evidence that women are experiencing individualized fractured identities while men are not.

Further reading

On stigma, see Goffman, E. (1963) *Stigma*. New York: Doubleday Anchor.
On health, see Annandale, E. and Hunt, K. (eds) (2000) *Gender Inequalities in Health*. Buckingham: Open University Press.
On crime and deviance, see Heidensohn, F. (1996) *Feminism and Criminology*. Buckingham: Open University Press; Pearson, G. (1983) *Hooligan*. London: Macmillan; Radford, J., Friedberg, M. and Harne, L. (eds) (2000) *Women, Violence and Strategies for Action*. Buckingham: Open University Press.
On race, see Cathcart, B. (2000) *The Case of Stephen Lawrence*. Harmondsworth: Penguin; Mason, D. (2000) *Race and Ethnicity in Modern Britain*, 2nd edn. Oxford: Oxford University Press.

7 Consumption, locality *and* identity

> We would have a house by the Bosphorous for the next half year, and
> contrast our emotions with those we had known by Burmoor Tarn.
> Think what a rich year of life that would make! How much we should
> have learnt from nature and from each other!
>
> (Gissing 1893/1980: 260)

In this quote, the 'hero' of *The Odd Women*, Everard Barfoot, is trying to per-
suade one of the heroines, Rhoda Nunn, to marry him. He offers life in two
locations – an exotic one in the mysterious East and a romantic one in the
English Lake District – partly as a metaphor for a marriage of equals, in
which both man and woman will have what they want. In this chapter,
issues of location, identity and consumption are addressed. I consider issues
of location in terms of neighbourhood, region, nation and class, together
with religion and politics. Issues of consumption around food are discussed.
Male and female differences in identity related to these topics are explored,
to see if men have kept to old loyalties while women have abandoned them.

It is a central tenet of the theory of post-modern society that men and
women define themselves by their consumption tastes (Lury 1997), rather
than by their role in production (i.e. by class). Thus many sociologists would
claim that men and women in 1893 and in 1951 were classifiable, and
classified themselves, by their relations to the system of production, whereas
in 2001 that is no longer the case.

In 1893, men and women of all social classes in Britain were exhorted
to have a global identity, as leaders of the British Empire (on which the sun
never set because there were colonies on every continent and in every ocean),
as well as a sense of British nationality. Below that was an identity as English, Irish, Scots or Welsh, and then an attachment to a county, city, town or
neighbourhood. There are no data on how far males and females differed in
their identification with the empire, with the constituent nations of Britain,
or with more local categories such as counties, towns or neighbourhoods. In
the 1890s, there were fears that refugees and asylum seekers were threaten-
ing 'the British way of life', as Jews from Russia and Eastern Europe arrived in
London, and there was prejudice against the Irish in many cities. However,

we do not know whether there were differences between the sexes in terms of these prejudices. For those women who wanted suffrage, of course, their identity as citizens was reduced by the nation's refusal to give them a vote, the most important symbol of full citizenship.

Except for the upper classes, the idea of identity being grounded in consumption was meaningless for men and women at this period: consumption 'choices' were constrained by poverty, locality and long working hours. Religious affiliations were more salient for both sexes in 1893 than we can imagine in 2001, and were enmeshed with political loyalties in ways that have also vanished. Methodist men and women were teetotal and supported the Liberal party; Roman Catholics were segregated in ways (such as schooling) throughout the UK that are now only noticeable in Northern Ireland. Our knowledge of any differences between the sexes, in terms of the patterns of these loyalties and sources of identity, is limited.

By 1951, the sources of identity were markedly different. The empire was ending (India and Pakistan became independent in 1948) and being an empire loyalist was to be part of a dying breed. The link between religious denomination and political party had weakened considerably, although less so in Wales, Scotland and Northern Ireland than in England. Women had been full voting citizens since 1929, although they still rarely sat on juries (chosen from lists of rate payers, not the electoral register), stood for parliament or took a civic role. Two wars had increased geographical mobility, but there is no evidence that men or women felt less loyalty to their region or neighbourhood. In 1951, there were many men and women whose primary identity was grounded in a workplace that was also a locality, such as mining villages, iron and steel towns, fishing ports and dockland neighbourhoods (for a summary of the many evocations of such communities, see Frankenberg 1966).

In this chapter, the parts played by consumption and locality in the lives of men and women over 25 today, compared with those of men and women in the 1890s and the early 1950s, are explored. If it were true that women had changed and men had not, the changes and stabilities should be displayed in the evidence on patterns of consumption and attachment to, or detachment from, locality. The identities of women and men should be thrown into relief by their patterns of consumption and their self-location in the contexts of neighbourhood, community, region, nation and 'global'. Let us see how such identities might be rehearsed at Kingsport.

Kingsport University 2006: Scene 7.1

It is St David's Day (1 March). Gwyneth Roberts, a librarian, has come to work with a large brooch bearing a leek and a daffodil. Her colleague in acquisitions, Roy Carbery, says: 'You're lucky to have an identity, white Englishmen have nothing unless they were born in Yorkshire'. Gwyneth thinks he's joking and then realizes he isn't. Roy really feels being English is a real problem for men.

Roy is not alone. Apart from the teenage boys studied by Mac an Ghaill (1994) described in Chapter 4, there is research by Nayak (1999) in

Birmingham and Back (1996) in London on young men who can only identify as being English by being racist. Nayak (1999: 76) argues that 'white working class masculinities' used to be 'virulently asserted in the space of the local'. When the 'masculine-affirmative process of manual labour' vanishes, 'investments in specific styles of whiteness' become a substitute. The young men he studied used National Front symbols as part of their identity. Mac an Ghaill, Nayak and Back all studied young working-class white men who felt it was hard to define any English identity except one that was racist, and espoused the political views of the National Front, British National Party and the violent fascist group Combat 18 (so-called because Adolph Hitler's two initials are the first and the eighth letters of the alphabet). In the years since Mac an Ghaill's study was published in 1994, many commentators have been struck by a 'crisis' in English identity. (The analysis of the motives of David Copeland, who bombed ethnic minority communities in Brick Lane and Brixton and gays in Soho, produced many such comments.) At a national level, one of the issues dividing the UK for the past 30 years has been the 'future of the union'; that is, the United Kingdom of Great Britain and Northern Ireland. Tom Nairn (1977) set out the debate, which was most violently embodied in Northern Ireland, but also mattered in Scotland and Wales. A minor note in the 1992 general election, the differences between the main political parties in 1997 concerning 'devolution' were one factor in an election result which left Wales and Scotland without any conservative MPs, and led to 'yes' votes for devolution in the following referenda.

The election of a government in 1997 that was pledged to create a Scottish parliament (McCrone 1992), a Welsh assembly (Osmond 1994; Morgan and Mungham 2000) and to try to resolve the 30 year conflict in Northern Ireland, even if that meant the end of the United Kingdom of Great Britain and Northern Ireland, created a public debate about 'Englishness' – the residual identity. It is clear that, for many English people, there is a reservoir of hatred and scorn for the Welsh, the Scots and the Irish of all religions. It is also clear that there is no easy way to express an Englishness that is not right-wing, racist, ethnocentric and *de facto* hostile to those who are not 'white'. Norman Tebbit's cricket test (if you support Sri Lanka, Pakistan or the West Indies you are not English) is not, as Marqusee (1994) shows vividly, really about cricket at all, but about racism. Similarly, when John Major talked of cricket, although he was actually describing the commercial pitches in cities like Worcester, Gloucester and Chelmsford, he appeared to be evoking cricket on a village green:

> Fifty years from now, Britain will still be the country of long shadows on county grounds, warm beer . . . old maids bicycling to holy communion through the morning mist.
>
> (Speech to the Conservative Group for Europe, 22 April 1993)

He was not only conjuring up a rural idyll, but an *English* one: from which many Scots (who prefer golf), Northern Irish (people of both religions) and Welsh (who play baseball) are excluded. Indeed, using cricket as a symbol of *Britain* was unwise and inaccurate. Apart from the large numbers of women bored by the game (although six of the most fanatical cricket enthusiasts

I know are women), cricket is predominantly English rather than British (although Scotland and Ireland have teams, and Glamorgan were county champions in 1997) *and* it has become global.

Wisden reports cricket from Afghanistan (whence it travelled with returning refugees from Pakistan) to Vanuatu and Kenya. The Netherlands and Denmark may soon be 'better' at it than England. Worse, cricket is a bad symbol of timelessness and continuity. The only way in which cricket is a good symbol of England is the perpetual sense of decline, crisis and impending doom expressed about cricket by the media (Marqusee 1994), which it shares with discourses about the family, women's morality, education, the behaviour of young people, street safety, community spirit and food that tastes of something (see Delamont 1999, 2000a). As Marqusee (1994) pointed out, cricket is a particularly nostalgia-ridden part of English culture. The Hornby and Barlow lauded in the 1898 poem had actually played 20 years before that, in the 1870s with W.G. Grace.

If John Major was inaccurate linking Britain to cricket, rather than England, even in England the speech was packed with 'minority' pleasures. Warm beer, being an old maid and cycling to church are not major pastimes or tastes. In England, most people under 50 would not recognize any of the items as relevant to their lives, or part of their identity.

There appear not to be any differences between the sexes in Wales, Scotland or Northern Ireland concerning loyalty to *those* identities: women, as deeply as men, seem to oppose or espouse Welsh devolution, the Scottish parliament, and the protestant or catholic causes in Northern Ireland. However, it *does* seem that the extreme form of English nationalism is predominantly a male preoccupation, at least in its violent manifestations. John Major's chocolate-box, calendar image of English identity may seem a long way from Combat 18 attacking Irishmen at a soccer international in Dublin, or the posturing of Mac an Ghaill's sad young men. The tragic consequences of a fierce adherence to an identity can be seen in the former Yugoslavia (Malcolm 1994; Bringa 1995; Friedman 1996) and in the turmoil caused in Greece by the resurgence of a separate 'Macedonian' identity (Karakasidou 1997; Mackridge and Yannakakis 1997). Opponents of devolution in the UK raise the spectre of Yugoslavia, although the Spanish example, especially the resurgence of Catalan identity (Woolard 1989), is a much more optimistic (and plausible) outcome.

In the next section, issues of identity are explored from the level of the neighbourhood to that of the nation.

Neighbourhood and community

One of the few aspects of contemporary British life which both sociologists and anthropologists have studied is the local neighbourhood or community. Several of the authors who have done so have straddled the two disciplines or collaborated across the divide. Frankenberg's (1966) synthesis of research on 'communities' in Britain, which moved from the most isolated rural hamlets to the most urban neighbourhood, was the benchmark. Since Frankenberg,

Cohen (1982, 1986) has put the most effort into systematic comparisons of different communities and explorations of belongingness. Bowie (1993), Trosset (1993), Chapman (1978, 1992a, 1992b) and Rapport (1993), among others, have studied community on the celtic fringe (Wales, Scotland) and in the remote rural areas of England (Cumbria) (for a review of these studies, see Rapport 2000). In these portraits of rural areas, both men and women appear similar in their attachment to their locality and the extent to which they gain their identity from their locality. Certainly in Rapport's study of a Cumbrian community, local men and women draw their identity with equal vehemence from that locality.

Although more people live in small towns, in suburbs, on estates peripheral to cities and in cities, not in remote rural areas, there are fewer studies of these localities both absolutely and in proportion to their role in the overall settlement pattern of the UK. That is, we know less about everyday life in such localities, and less about how far such localities provide a sense of identity for men or women. When Dennis *et al.* (1956) studied a mining community in Yorkshire, both the miners and the women in their families (mothers, wives, daughters, sisters) drew their identity from that mining village. Dicks (1996, 2000), who has studied former mining areas in England and Wales, has argued that 'women's position within a declining labour market is potentially problematic even where men find alternative employment' (Dicks 1996: 40). Many of Dicks' female respondents felt that *their* community had gone with the pit, and that their lives had got much worse. Dick concluded that: 'It is women who will, it seems, be bearing the major burdens in this post-industrial social landscape' (p. 42).

Explorations of urban neighbourhoods are rarer: the shadow of Willmot and Young's Bethnal Green is so deep, little subsequently has grown in it. Back (1996) is an exception, with his skilful evocation of life in a London suburb. Some of the best insights come from the sociology of education, where a desire to find out how parents 'choose' state schools for their children has given us an insight into the class-based nature of localism. The work of Gewirtz *et al.* (1995) on parental choice of secondary school in London in the 1990s found that issues of locality and identity were central to that choice for working-class parents, especially the unskilled (pp. 50–53). Using Cremin's (1979) idea of a 'functional community', and Harvey's (1989) idea of 'spaces of representation', Gewirtz *et al.* (1995: 52) argued that:

> Where transport deprivation leads to social isolation and segregation of particular social groups in particular localities, *social enclaves* are created. The existence of such enclaves reinforces the importance of *the local.*

In the areas of London studied by Gewirtz and her colleagues, this strong positive feeling for the locality led parents to choose the neighbourhood school, however 'poor' it was in terms of exam results, teacher turnover, truancy or leaking buildings. This fierce localism was shared by men and women and was class-based but not differentiated by gender. Middle- and upper middle-class parents did not value the physical proximity of a secondary school at all and appeared not to have the same sense of physical community or neighbourhood. These data were on families with children aged 10 and 11,

but the same phenomenon has been found in South Wales at the next trans-
ition, from school to higher education. Working-class parents of adolescents
wanted them to attend a higher education institution near home, however
lowly its status in terms of research or teaching. Middle- and upper-class
families wanted the 'best' higher education their children could get, and valued
leaving home as a landmark in their children's independence and autonomy
(Pugsley 1998).

This had been reported in Swansea in the 1960s by Diana Leonard
Barker (1972), where 'keeping close' was seen as desirable by parents, who
were concerned to keep their adult children with them. This value system
turned out to be influencing choice of university in the 1990s (Pugsley 1998).
In both eras, there are strong attachment factors (of identity and family
solidarity) *and* fears about the danger of life among strangers. Working-class
parents said that they would be too anxious about their children if they left
Cardiff and lived among strangers. There is a sex difference here, in that
parents are more worried about girls, but that is less striking than the gener-
alized value of 'keeping close'.

Similar points are made about unemployed men in the English Midlands
(Canaan 1996; Nayak 1999), whose locality was a territory that gave them a
(working-class) identity. Canaan (1996: 118) argued that 'local territory was
particularly important for those lacking the cultural capital to move far from
it both literally and figuratively'. Work by Coffey *et al.* (1998) on unemployed young men in South Wales found similar features, recapitulated when
they took a holiday in Spain. Away from their valley they lost all sense of
identity, until they recreated it by finding a place to hang out that was 'the
same' as the bus shelter they loitered by in the 'home' valley.

This differentiates them from the middle classes or upper middle classes
of both sexes, who occupy what Lash and Urry (1994) call economies of
signs and space (see also Connell 1993). Lash and Urry contrast the lives of
affluent, educated people with jobs that are enhanced by global telecommunications and who are not tied to a locality, with those of the underclass
who are increasingly trapped in their neighbourhood. A working class left
high and dry by the loss of heavy industry, trapped in a locality without
work, characterizes not just inner-city areas, but also communities once dependent on mining (Dicks 1996) and on iron and steel (Harris 1987).

Lash and Urry (1994) argued that, with the end of localized heavy
industry and the rise of post-industrialism, an underclass has developed,
isolated in the inner cities, the peripheral council estates and the rural areas.
Men and women in the middle and upper classes, whose social networks are
founded on the phone, the Internet, the car and the plane, live in social
spaces that are geographically dispersed but emotionally and intellectually
'close'. Their thesis is captured by the title of their book *Economies of Signs
and Space*: for the educated, the computer-literate and the mobile, identity is
not based on attachment to a neighbourhood or physical locality. Nowhere
do Lash and Urry suggest that there are gender differences in identity in
these new economies of signs and space. Feminists have proposed that women
experience towns and cities very differently from men (e.g. Wilson 1991), but
this does not mean that they construct their *identity* differently.

It is arguable that Lash and Urry, like John Major, are describing the English rather than the rest of Britain. The Welsh, the Scots and people of both religions in Northern Ireland of all social classes may be less enamoured of abandoning neighbourhood and locality as primary sources of identity, because they are bound up with regional or national identities *as* Welsh, Scots, 'Irish' or Unionist, than the English educated middle classes. Certainly this could be argued from the research of David McCrone and his various collaborators, who have explored the nature of Scottish identity with the growth of 'heritage' as a form of consumption.

Identity and heritage

McCrone *et al.* (1995) link the rise of modern Scottish nationalism and identity with the rise of a Scottish heritage industry. Suiting their research to this belief, the team have studied the heritage industry, life members of the National Trust for Scotland, and members of the arts elite and the landed elite (McCrone *et al.* 1998). Heritage is an 'intensely personal matter' (McCrone *et al.* 1995: 165) combined with 'a broad sense of nationalism' (p. 166). This sense of Scottishness is strong and growing stronger. By 1997, 61 per cent of Scots said they felt more Scottish than British and 48 per cent said they had more in common with a Scot of another social class than an English person of the same class. These findings run counter to the theories of Lash and Urry, for it is precisely the consumers of heritage high culture who should be abandoning a parochial celtic identity to live in the new economy of signs and space. An outsider to Scotland might argue that privileging national identity over class identity is romantic nonsense, because class and its associated matters of life chance, wealth and taste mean that a Scots lawyer and a Welsh doctor have more in common than a Scots lawyer has with an unemployed member of the Glasgow underclass as personified by Rab C. Nesbitt, but the *myth* is itself interesting. If Scots are claiming the priority of nationality above class, it is an interesting *claim*. Good social science pays attention to people's statements, even when we doubt their veracity. In the unlikely bestseller of 1997, *Courtesans and Fishcakes*, James Davidson (1997) writes: 'What is interesting about Foucault's work is the realisation that misrepresentations are just as interesting as representations, and even more useful, when you can identify them, are outrageous lies' (p. xxii).

Picking up just such a misrepresentation, McCrone and his colleagues discuss the rise of the new Scottish anthem. When Scots at sporting occasions sing of 'The wee bit hill and glen' defended against 'Proud Edwards's army' (the English) in the anthem *Flower of Scotland*, most of them are urban office workers singing a modern song, not rural highland soldiers celebrating a medieval battle in a 'traditional' folk song. Yet, as McCrone *et al.* (1995: 204) note, the song 'may make weak poetry but strong politics'. 'The iconography leaks' so it can be used radically. Parallel work on Welsh identities can be found in Thompson *et al.* (1999). The referenda on devolution for Wales and Scotland in 1979 and 1997 provide data on whether men and women differ

Table 7.1   Sex and referenda votes 1979 and 1997

	1979				1997			
	Yes (%)	No (%)	Did not vote (%)	n	Yes (%)	No (%)	Did not vote (%)	n
Scottish men	40	34	26	319	58	14	27	291
Scottish women	34	41	25	329	53	19	26	385
Welsh men	19	52	28	—	34	30	35	293
Welsh women	15	44	39	—	28	31	40	393

Note: All figures have been rounded.
Adapted from Surridge and McCrone (1999) and Wyn Jones and Trystan (1999); unpublished data supplied by R. Wyn Jones.

in their attitudes to it. Table 7.1 reflects the votes in the referenda broken down by gender.

There are no statistically significant sex differences in Table 7.1. However, it is clear that Welsh women were the least likely to vote in both 1979 and 1997, whereas Scottish women came out in the same proportion as men. Women in both countries, like men, were more enthusiastic about devolution in 1997 than they had been in 1979. It appears from Table 7.1 that the Scots are more enthusiastic than the Welsh about devolution and that men are more enthusiastic than women. There may be problems for men in finding an English identity, but there is no such problem for men in Wales or Scotland. This may be partly because of sport: men in Wales and Scotland may combine sporting loyalties with 'national' identity more readily than women.

Sport and 'heritage' may seem remote from many people's lives. In the next section, I move through the data on food and drink on to the other 'big' issues in forming people's identities in contemporary Britain – religion, politics and social class. Issues of identity come much closer to everyone's lives in the area of food and drink.

Food and drink

Food and drink may seem to be very poor topics to relate to identity for either sex. In fact, choices about types of food and drink mark out people of different religions, political beliefs and social classes, as well as different races and nationalities very neatly. Eating haggis and mashed swede or turnip on 29 January to celebrate the life and work of Burns is a very Scottish act (see Delamont 1994, Chapter 2 for a fuller discussion of this issue). We are fortunate in having high-quality, up-to-date research on food choices in contemporary Britain from which we can learn a good deal about gender, identity and social change. Murcott (1998) contains the results of a large research programme, *The Nation's Diet*, including projects on newly established households, on African Caribbean and white families in London, on rural Wales, on older people, and on Italians and South Asians in Glasgow. What people eat, whether it is prepared from scratch, bought ready to microwave, carried home from a takeaway or eaten in a pub or cafe, is an important element in their sense of self: their race, their religion, their respectability. Let us go back to Kingsport.

Kingsport 2006: Scene 6.2, March 1st

Roy Carbery gives a lift home to Roxana Habib, a new graduate librarian who lives with her family in the next street to his house. Thinking about Gwyneth, who said she was having lava bread and bacon for her tea because it is St. David's Day, he asks Roxana what she expects to have for supper. Roxana laughs: 'If Dad's home, Mum will have cooked curry and chapatas. If he's working, the kids will have argued for something English'.

Roy, intrigued, asks 'Such as?', knowing Roxana has two younger sisters living at home who are still at school, and a male cousin of 10 whose mother is in hospital staying with them. 'Pizza', says Roxana, 'or lasagna, or fish fingers and chips'. Roy laughs, thinking how his father, a Durham miner, would have refused to have pizza or lasagna in his house, regarding them as 'foreign muck'. He was a meat and potatoes man, Roy recalls, planning his own supper of seared tuna and stir fried vegetables.

This scenario is grounded in the research. Valentine (1999) reports a study of 67 people from twelve households in Yorkshire. She argues that food choices were one of the ways that families and households established and maintained their identities, whether religious, cultural or sub-cultural. Her informants included a Muslim couple who use food, together with sending their children to after-school Islam classes at the Mosque, to maintain their cultural identity, and vegetarians self-consciously creating a new, meat-free identity for themselves.

Valentine's study of food choices at home is complemented by research on eating out. Warde *et al.* (1999) report the outcome of interviews in 30 households in Preston, followed by a survey of 1001 people over 16 in London, Bristol and Preston, on eating out. Choice of cuisine when eating outside the home and buying takewaways was related to class, education and ethnicity, but not gender. Forty-eight per cent of those interviewed had not eaten in any ethnic restaurant in the previous year, and 27 per cent did not eat 'ethnic' takeaway food. The more educated people (those with degrees), the wealthier and the younger were more likely to have eaten in 'ethnic' restaurants. The Londoners were more likely to have eaten Indian, Chinese, Italian and other ethnic food in restaurants than those in Preston and Bristol, but less likely to eat in pubs. Members of ethnic minorities avoid 'British' food outlets. The interrelations between food, drink, religion and identity are explored in Delamont (1994).

In the Kingsport scenario, Roxana's identity is not, of course, just a matter of food. The scenario contrasts generations as well as a British Muslim household with that of a non-practising Christian household. As church attendance among Christians in Britain has declined, it is easy to believe that religion is no longer a potent source of identity compared to 1893 or 1951. This would be a mistake. For some women and men, identity is closely tied to religion. Among Christians in Britain, active, regular attenders at services are more likely to be women, especially women over 65, than men. Attendance at mainstream Christian churches (Anglican, Roman Catholic, Methodist, Presbyterian, etc.) is in steady decline, as is participation in life-cycle events (baptisms, confirmations, weddings) and the numbers of people claiming to be members. In 1970, 9.1 million adults were members of a mainstream Christian Church; in 1995, only 6.4 million were (*Social Trends* 1999: 220). However, about 65 per cent of adults state they believe in Christianity, although they do not take part in any religious activities or pay any church a subscription. Among Christians, women are more active than men: about half the women in Britain attend church at least once a year (compared to a third of men). Women over 65 are the most regular church attenders. For these women, being a churchgoer is a source of identity.

For women, the gradual decline in church adherence is associated with a fall in membership of the church-related women's organizations. The Mothers Union and the Church of Scotland Women's Guild both lost about half their members between 1971 and 1987 (*Social Trends* 1999: 175). Most of the other women-only leisure organizations, such as the Townswomen's Guild and the Scottish Women's Rural Institutes, also report declining memberships. Compared with 1951, it appears that fewer women in 1999 find their sense of identity in church or in women-only philanthropic and charitable organizations. Many of these groups were founded after 1893, as part of the movement of women into the public sphere. The Townswomen's Guild, for example, was set up after 1918 to teach urban women how to vote wisely. As women's employment grows, reducing their time for organizations, fewer women seem to seek an identity in the single-sex voluntary sector.

Turning to the many non-Christian religions, Judaism is also in decline. In contrast to Christianity and Judaism, Islam, Sikhism and Hinduism are all growing. In 2001, there are at least 600,000 Muslims, 350,000 Sikhs and 155,000 Hindus (up from 130,000, 100,000 and 80,000 respectively in 1970) in the UK. These are growing not just because of ethnic minority populations, but also through conversions, and are different from Christianity in that *men* are actively involved and the participants are younger than 65. It seems that a non-Christian religious identity fits into male identity better than a Christian one does. As these three religions were barely present in the Britain of 1893 or the Britain of 1951, it is not possible to see if women have changed while men have not in relation to an Islamic, Sikh or Hindu identity.

Sport of some kind is a central part of identity for many people, especially if the particular sport can be tied to an ethnicity, a religion or a region (McClancy 1996). Werbner (1996), for example, explores the ways in which young British Pakistani men in Greater Manchester are British but are simultaneously supporters of Pakistan at cricket ('If you cut my wrists, green blood will come out').

Religious identity is related to racial and regional cultures. Christian adherence is very different across the various regions of the UK. Active participation is much higher in Northen Ireland than anywhere else, and somewhat higher in Scotland and Wales than in England. Political allegiance can give people an identity and, for some people, this is important. Adherence to either a mainstream political party such as *Plaid Cymru* or a campaigning movement such as Friends of the Earth can be a source of identity and provide a sense of belonging. Membership of mainstream political parties is in decline, however, and apart from voting at general elections, most adults of both sexes are not involved in political activity. However, there is an association between people's idea about their social class, their voting patterns and their attitude to trade unions which has not shifted in the last 50 years. There is still a strong sense in which people feel a class membership, and their class membership is related to how they vote and to whether they feel trade unions are on the side of the 'good guys' or are the enemy.

Class: the final frontier

The years of conservative governments under Thatcher and Major (1979–97) saw a rhetorical attack on the existence of social class in Britain, a sustained attack on sociology and funds for sociological research that reduced our knowledge about class, and changes in the economic system and the labour market which are the basis of class. None of this, however, means that social class has vanished. Class inequalities in health, educational achievement, housing, diet and lifestyle persist. So, too, does class as a source of identity, as part of our sense of who we are and where we belong. Every time anyone speaks, their accent, dialect and vocabulary locate them in a region, a class, a lifestyle. Scots women go out for 'messages' rather than going shopping, and then, if they are working-class, cook dinner at twelve noon and tea at five-thirty; however, if upper class, lunch is served at one-thirty and dinner at eight. When different classes eat at different times and label their meals differently, these are surface 'markers' of much deeper issues.

Grounded in the occupational structure, class identity is still strong. Skeggs (1997) provides the clearest account of how working-class women 'know' that they are working class and what that means. Take this young woman reflecting on the middle-class girls she despised at school:

> When we were at school we used to beat them up. We'd wait for them coming down our way going home from school. They frighten dead easy. But it's like now they're the ones getting their own back. They have money and cars and we're still hanging round here.
>
> (Therese, 1989 in Skeggs 1997: 92)

Another of Skegg's informants, Wendy, describes being in Manchester's grandest department store and being looked at by a woman:

> If looks could kill. Like we were only standing there ... She just looked. It was like it was her place and we didn't belong there. And you know what? we all just walked away ... Can you imagine? Well and truly put in our place ... You feel better staying around here.
>
> (Skeggs 1997: 92)

This sense of 'knowing your place', which is both a physical place and a class location, explains the lack of working-class applications to Oxbridge and many other self-segregations. Frazer's (1989) study of talk in an upper-class girls school provides the view from above to complement that of Skegg's informants.

Class may not be explicitly mentioned quite as frequently as it once was, but that does not mean that it is gone from people's sense of self. The working classes are subject to symbolic violence in contemporary Britain, in exactly the way Wendy describes, and such symbolic violence impacts on the sense of self (see Bradley 1997).

However, what is clear from most of the research done in Britain since 1945 is that women's sense of self, and the core of their identity, is predicted on issues centred on respectability and femininity. These are partly class-related and partly tied to money, but also depend on other matters. For most women, identity depends on drawing lines between herself as a respectable woman and others who are not, between herself as feminine and others who are not; that is, between herself and those who are 'other'. The 'other' can be sexually promiscuous, financially profligate, wrongly dressed, a bad mother, a lesbian, a feminist, a snob or whatever, but she is the negative stereotype against which women measure themselves. McDonald (1989) shows this very clearly in her work on rural Brittany, as does Skeggs (1997) in her longitudinal case study of young women in the North West of England, and Pilcher (1998) for South Wales. As Skeggs (1997: 1) argues, 'Respectability is one of the most ubiquitous signifiers of class. It informs how we speak, who we speak to, how we classify others, . . . and how we know who we are (or are not)'. Her informants valued their respectability: their clothing, the cleaniless of their homes, the dress and behaviour of their children, and their friends. For working-class women, it is all they have; for women in other classes, it is important too.

Verdict

Have women's sources of identity changed while those of men have stayed the same? No. If anything, it is the reverse. Women's identity is grounded in class, femininity and respectability; men's has been changed by post-industrial restructuring.

Further reading

Bradley, H. (1997) *Fractured Identities*. Cambridge: Polity Press.
Mason, D. (2000) *Race and Ethnicity in Modern Britain*, 2nd end. Oxford: Oxford University Press.

8 Work *and* identity: *the* indignities *of* labour

> A womanly occupation means, practically, an occupation that a man disdains.
>
> (Gissing 1893/1980: 135)

One of the central themes of *The Odd Women* is the misery women face if they cannot earn a living, especially when poor wages and terrible working conditions are common in the few occupations open to respectable females, such as shop work, being a governess or a 'companion'. The heroines Mary Barfoot and Rhoda Nunn are trying in a practical way to train women to work in 'male' jobs, such as book-keeping, so they can support themselves and stay respectable. In this quote, Rhoda Nunn is dismissing the Victorian division of labour, in which women's work – whether manual or white collar – was sharply divided from men's, badly paid and exploitative. This chapter explores what we know about women, men and work, both paid and unpaid, in contemporary Britain, to determine whether women's orientation to labour has changed while men's has not.

This chapter compares the working lives of women and men over 25 today, contrasting 2001 with the 1890s and the immediate post-war period. The central focus of the chapter is paid employment, rather than voluntary work and work done in households for love. Any discussion of employment in contemporary Britain is coloured by a set of beliefs that casualization, contract work, out-sourcing and part-time working have swept away the 'career', the job for life. However, it is not at all clear that those trends are as prevalent as they are believed to be.

Meadows (1999) challenges the belief that the UK labour market has changed all that much since 1975. She argues that, in 1980, 21 per cent of all employees (and 42 per cent of working women) worked part-time. By 1995, this had risen to 25 per cent, but has not moved since; most of the increase was due to students doing part-time work because of the abolition of grants. In 1995, there were nearly a million part-time workers, 90 per cent of whom were on permanent contracts.

In 1975, the average job lasted 6 years and 1 month; in 1999, it was 5 years and 6 months. So, overall, there has not been a dramatic decrease in length of employment. However, people under 24 go through more jobs before settling down in their late twenties: a school leaver or graduate in 1999 can expect eleven jobs in their working life, whereas someone retiring in 1999 had seven. Meadows also found a small rise in contract working (7 per cent today compared with 5 per cent in 1979) and that most people (70 per cent) on contracts move into permanent jobs after 3–6 months. A 1998 survey found that 88 per cent of workers felt secure in their jobs; that's reasonable when 5 per cent lose their job in a 'good' year and 7.5 per cent do so in a 'bad' one.

Bearing Meadow's work in mind, we can examine male and female orientations to the labour market in 1893 and in 1951. In 1893, women did not share one single orientation to paid employment. In the upper class, many *men* did little or no work, and paid employment for women was socially unacceptable. Ladies could do voluntary work and could run the family's estates and households, but not take paid posts. In the upper middle and middle classes, most men and women expected wives to be full-time dependents, running their houses and rearing children. However, widows and spinsters were a problem; for the previous 40 years, a minority movement had campaigned for reasonably paid occupations to be opened up for them, so that they could earn enough to be self-supporting (see Vicinus 1985; Delamont 1989). Gissing's heroines are involved in this movement. So, among *ladies* there was a minority of females with careers, whose primary identity was that of a school teacher, a doctor, a lecturer in a teacher training college or a university, or a nurse.

The first woman to qualify as a doctor in Britain, Elizabeth Garret Anderson, did so in 1865, followed by a group who forced Edinburgh to teach them in its medical school. By 1874, women had their own medical school in London and the most successful were becoming surgeons and gynaecologists (Moberly Bell 1953; Blake 1990). Women were not able to be dentists until 1895, vets until 1922, solicitors until 1922, barristers until 1922 and accountants until 1919. The Sex Disqualification (Removal) Act of 1919 removed barriers to women's entry to most professional occupations.

In the skilled working class, the highly paid trades were barred to women, and the men took pride in earning enough to support a family. A wife who was not employed was a symbol of male prowess and respectability. Daughters could work between school and marriage, but were not expected to make that work their main source of identity. We know relatively little about how such respectable women in the artisan class felt about this. Below the skilled working classes were 70 per cent of the population, living in families where everyone who could earn did so, in paid employment, in self-employment or both. Here a woman could be a breadwinner, be skilful and be proud of her skills, or be resentful of back-breaking labour that was poorly regarded and badly paid. Here identity would be grounded in a mixture of ideas about the respectability of the home, the paid work done, the locality and the employment status of the husband.

In general, therefore, few women in 1893 would have based the core of their identity on their paid employment. The minority who did so were spinsters, widows, feminists or some combination of the three. Women's participation in a wide variety of non-traditional jobs in the 1914–18 and the 1939–45 wars was short-lived: peace came and the women left gratefully or were driven out of the 'men's' jobs. In 1951, many women in all social classes had been in paid employment and most had been educated to some extent. However, in 1951, the ideological climate was hostile to married women, especially mothers, having paid employment outside the home. (Taking lodgers, or doing other people's washing was more acceptable.) Equal pay was almost unknown, many occupations were closed to women and others had marriage bars. Spinsters were expected to support themselves and widows might need to work, but men were expected to support their households. The welfare state brought in by the Labour government after 1945 was predicated on stable marriages in which men supported women and children with wages or benefits. Relatively few women, mostly spinsters, drew their major source of identity from their paid employment.

Britain in 2001 is very different, insofar as the participation of married women and especially mothers of dependent children in paid employment is concerned. The underlying economy is also different, with a steady decline in the manufacturing sector and in manual jobs, matched by growth in service and office jobs and so a rise in white-collar occupations. The issue for this chapter is whether these changes have (a) altered women's attitudes to, and behaviour in, the labour market and (b) *not* altered men's attitudes to, and behaviour in, the labour market. It is inappropriate to review all the research on women and employment, because Crompton (1997) and Rees (1992, 1998, 1999) focused entirely on women and work in Britain and the European Union, and the aim here is not to recapitulate their coverage. Instead, I focus on the change and/or stability of men's and women's attitudes to paid employment.

There are two interrelated debates about the impact of married women's increased labour market participation on British society that are germane to the central topic of this book. Some writers claim that married women's entry to the labour market is causing widespread social disruption and should be reduced; that is, they want a return to the labour market of 1951. Simultaneously, there is a claim that most sociologists who have conducted research on women in paid employment and its consequences have produced bad, ideologically biased publications that promulgate lies about women's attitudes to work.

The integrity of the published research on women and paid employment is absolutely central to this chapter and, indeed, to the whole book. The changes in the labour market are pivotal to all debates about whether women have changed, so it is essential that the data are reliable and valid. McRae (1999: 56) summarizes the changes as follows:

One highly visible outcome of the switch to services has been a shift in the gender composition of the workforce. In the twenty years from 1975 ... men's employment fell and women's employment grew. Throughout most of the 1970s, fewer than one in ten men of working age, but about forty per cent of married women ... were economically inactive – not in work or seeking work. Between 1979 and 1997 the number of economically inactive men doubled from 1.4 to 2.8 million, while the number of economically inactive women fell by one million to 4.6 million . . . By 1997 women accounted for nearly one in every two people in the labour force.

The issue of whether or not women's participation in the paid labour market has damaged men (Dench 1996; Fukuyama 1999) and caused social disruption is addressed later in this chapter and again in Chapter 9. Before that claim can be discussed, the attack on the integrity of the sociologists who had studied women and employment by Catherine Hakim (1995) must be addressed.

The polemical attack on conventional sociological accounts of gender and work by Hakim (1995) in her 'Five feminist myths about women's employment' article will form the core of this chapter. To dramatize the central issues, let us start at Kingsport University.

Kingsport University 2006: Scene 8.1

Grace Pinker, an engineering student, is in the pub with her tutorial group: Tom Sawdon, Eddie Smithers, David Shirley, Costas Marcoulidas and Ibrahim Maazouzi. They discuss the practical class they've just had, in which the senior technician, Reg Aythorne, had told Grace he 'didn't know why she wanted to do engineering', 'it wasn't suitable for a girl' and 'he wouldn't want his daughter' doing a course like hers. 'The only girl' in a section full of men, and 'most of them Arabs and Pakis'. Grace says that the 'poor man' was clearly upset because of the flu epidemic which had left him short-staffed and 'he probably didn't mean it'. Costas, a Greek Cypriot from London, says Grace should complain about Reg, not sympathize. Eddie argues that the 'real world' of engineering will be full of 'much worse' men than Reg and Grace 'might as well get used to it'. Ibrahim, an Algerian, says someone might tell Reg that lots of engineers in Egypt are women, and Eddie retorts that Reg would just say Egypt was a rubbish country.

Here all the main divisions in the labour market are displayed. The students, *en route* to occupations in the top social class, are distanced from Reg, the working-class technician. The 'proper' spheres of women versus men, of caucasians versus orientals, of natives versus immigrants or foreigners, and of cultural relativities versus ethnocentrism are all displayed. Grace's response to Reg's views is fairly typical of women's reactions to sexist critics, sympathizing with the critic and explaining the attack away as due to stress, problems and so on, rather than challenging them (see Caplan 1993). When a madman, Mare Lepine, murdered fourteen women at Montreal's École Polytechnique shouting 'You're all feminists, I hate feminists', it was in the engineering department and many of the women victims were engineering students. There was no evidence at all that any of them was a feminist.

It is against the background of a labour market in the UK which is believed to be changing rapidly (because of de-industrialization and globalization) but which is characterized by segregations of sex, race and class background, that the debate over the arguments put forward by Hakim needs to be examined. The research on women and the labour market (Rees 1992) was aggressively challenged by Hakim (1995, 1996). She erupted in some anger against what she claimed was an ideologically charged, counter-factual consensus about women and work, which stereotyped women as victims of a patriarchal labour market. Hakim (1995) claimed to have found 'five feminist myths' about women and employment, using 'myth' in the popular sense of untruth, or lie, rather than its normal social science usage (Leach 1970). (Serious anthropologists use myth in a technical sense, to mean any story that is told to provide a charter or justification for action, any explanation for the present state of affairs.)

Hakim's five lies were:

1 That women's employment has been rising during the twentieth century, especially since 1945, and particularly the employment of married women
2 That women's orientation and commitment to work has become the same as men's
3 That a lack of child care is the main barrier to women's employment
4 That part-time workers (most of whom are women) are exploited in poor-quality jobs
5 That the job stability of female employees equals that of males.

Hakim states that feminist sociologists who believe these five lies assert them in the face of the evidence, and are thus able to blame a patriarchal labour market for women's labour market position and lower wages. Hakim, in contrast, argues that *none* of the above is true, the labour market cannot be characterized as patriarchal and that women have not changed their orientations to work or the family.

She expanded her attack on the five lies in the following way. Hakim (1995) argued that there were no more women in the labour force in 1971 than there had been in 1851, but rather than single women in full-time work, there were married women in part-time work. Only since the mid-1980s has women's employment started to rise. Hakim believes that women work only because they have financial needs, not because work is central to their identities. Hakim claims that when surveys of employers reveal them to prefer male workers, because men are believed to have higher commitment and less absenteeism, feminists see this as prejudice, when it is in fact an accurate response to women's lower commitment to their job.

Hakim (1995) then dismisses arguments that women are prevented from taking full-time employment by a lack of child care, claiming instead that half of all women prioritize child-rearing, prefer part-time work, and do not seek or desire labour market engagement. She proceeds from this to dismiss arguments that part-time workers (mainly women) are severely dis-advantaged (that is, in terms of pay and conditions) in the labour market. Finally, she argues that women have lower attachment to their work than men do. If Hakim's arguments are correct, then it would be absurd to argue that women had changed since 1893 or 1951. In Hakim's belief system,

women have not changed their attitudes at all, and any changes in behaviour are due to financial hardship.

Before exploring the accuracy of Hakim's ideas, which run counter
to those of McRae (1999) set out earlier in the chapter, it is important to
recognize what kind of social scientist Hakim is. Part of her hostility to
'feminist' sociology (which she sees as ideological rather than objective)
stems from her attachment to a positivist, survey-based sociology. She is not
a relativist or a postmodernist in her methods, and she does not pay attention to the arguments about reflexive modernity or post-industrialism as new
forms of social order. She grounds her argument in her faith in the research
methods of positivist sociology:

> Random samples for interview surveys, double-blind experiments, studies
> of experimenter effects and self-fulfilling predictions among researchers
> (which) ensure that the research results are more than simple corrob-
> orations of the researcher's prejudices.
>
> (Hakim 1995: footnote 12)

At root, therefore, she only believes in the data from surveys and that sociology is 'in the truth business'. There is, however, a problem with a blind
adherence to such positivist methods. Data collected in such ways may omit
the experiential: the ways in which men and women experience paid employment, family life, parenthood and identity.

Hakim's (1995) deliberately provocative piece, in which her most
savage attacks were made on unnamed and uncited 'British scholars', produced a joint response from ten researchers (men and women; Ginn *et al.*
1996) and a counterclaim from one feminist (Breugel 1996). The 'ten' coun-
tered Hakim's argument with different statistics from different surveys,
or varying interpretations of the same data. That is, they too were positivists, and they argued with Hakim on the basis of similar sets of data, dis-
agreeing only about what the material meant. Breugel (1996) challenged her
epistemology.

Hakim's (1996) subsequent book elaborated her beliefs, arguing that
'women' was no longer a useful category. Instead, she argued, women need
to be seen as *either* part of the majority of their sex who choose to prioritize
their family life and only work for secondary earnings *or* as part of a minority who have chosen to concentrate on paid employment and behave 'like
men'. She used the terms 'grateful slaves' and 'self-determining' for these
groups and received favourable media coverage for the book.

If Hakim is right about the 'grateful slaves' being the vast majority of
women, then the pessimistic authors who believe the employment of women
is destroying men, families and British society are misguided. Most women
have not changed and society is safe. If she is wrong, then women's labour
market orientation has changed and the social consequences of that change
need exploration.

There are two issues that need to be disentangled here: (1) How good
are the data that Hakim and her critics are using? (2) Do other data produce
a different picture?

The data

Hakim depends primarily on large-scale survey data. One of the central concerns about such data has to be whether the people surveyed were offering answers about what they thought were ideal patterns (what ought to be happening) or what they actually did (what is happening in their lives) and, if the latter, how far they were reporting *accurately* on what they did. People often tell survey researchers about social norms and ideal worlds. Huber and Spitze (1983) found that while men and women held clear views about what *ought* to happen in the areas of sex roles, their own lives were lived at variance with these ideals. Women who believed mothers should stay out of paid employment held full-time jobs and women who believed mothers should take paid employment were full-time homemakers. The cognitive dissonance was explained by personal circumstances: 'we don't like it, but we have a big mortgage'; 'I don't think its right, but we can't manage'; 'I want to work, but there's no decent childcare nearby'. Hakim does not cite this work and shows no understanding of such subtleties. Nor does Hakim cite Rees (1992), whose detailed research on women in the labour market reveals that survey data alone cannot begin to deal with issues like 'attachment' to the labour market, nor employers' attitudes to male or female employees (Rees and Fielder 1992).

Longitudinal studies of cohorts of women challenge Hakim's categorization. Skeggs (1997) and Procter and Padfield (1999) both conclude that women's employment patterns develop in an interactive relationship between employment on the one hand and personal goals and expectations on the other. The barriers to career equality for women, for mothers and for carers highlighted by scholars such as Rees (1992, 1998) impact on this interactive relationship.

Detailed analysis of gender and specific labour markets support the idea of the heterogeneity of women workers, but divide them by age and qualifications rather than ideology. This heterogeneity is amplified by changing context of employment in the UK. The birth rate in Britain has declined sharply, so that most women have only one or two children: this changes the meaning of 'working mothers'. De-industrialization means that the employment available is more frequently in service industries, where 'people skills' are needed. Adkins (1995) points out how the growth of the tourist, heritage and leisure industries, all of which depend for their profitability on the quality of the human interaction, produce jobs for women, who are believed to be better at 'emotion work' or 'front-line consumer service work'. About 70 per cent of those employed in catering and hotels are women. Changes in European Union legislation are altering the balance of advantage to employers in employing young and old, male and female (Rees 1998). Walby (1997) concludes that the legislative changes of the past 30 years have improved the position of women in employment, that younger women with credentials have much better employment chances than either older women or coevals who lack credentials, and that domestic duties are of less importance to younger, better qualified women. Walby's blend of different types of data, and her sensitivity to variations between local labour markets, is a more productive way forward. Rees (1999) offers just such a careful analysis of women in Wales. Research published since Hakim (1995), such as that of Jacobs (1997), supports the claims that the labour market has not adapted to maximize the female labour force. Jacobs uses survey data from the Social Change and Economic Life Initiative (SCELI), conducted in 1986 in six urban labour markets (Swindon, Rochdale, Northampton, Kirkcaldy, Coventry and Aberdeen), of 3415 women. Most women who return to the labour market after childbirth are disadvantaged and their skills under-utilized in the labour market. They re-enter employment in lower-status, more poorly paid and part-time jobs. Only a minority of highly qualified women who returned very quickly to full-time posts did not suffer from becoming mothers. Jacobs does not argue for different orientations among the mothers between 'grateful slaves' and 'self-determining' women, but stresses structural barriers to all but a tiny minority of highly qualified women.

At the same time as Hakim (1995, 1996) was arguing that the academic orthodoxy on women and paid work was wrong, there was a good deal of anxiety about the disappearance of male jobs, especially unskilled and semi-skilled male jobs. If male self-respect and identity were based on their occupation, what happens to men when there are no jobs, or only degrading jobs, or work they associate with women? There are three sub-strands to this argument. Some commentators focus on young men without skills or credentials whose passage to adulthood – and adult responsibility – is disrupted by the lack of jobs (Wallace 1987; Riseborough 1993a). Others worry about the health of unemployed men, because prolonged unemployment is associated with mental and physical deterioration (Acheson 1998). A third group worry that the whole society will be engulfed by lawlessness and degradation, because males have 'lost' their roles as breadwinners, hunters, *men* (Dench 1996; Fukuyama 1999). Dench and Fukuyama propose that women should leave the labour market so men can experience full employment.

It is true that the increase in married women's work between 1975 and 1997 has come from households where the man already had a job. Sixty per cent of families with dependent children have two wages coming in today, while 10 per cent have no wage-earner. The former figure has grown since 1984, the latter has stayed the same. However, it is not clear that women leaving the labour market would help young unskilled males, men with health problems, or restore masculine self-esteem. The jobs that unskilled men did have vanished with de-industrialization and mechanization. Women have not taken them; they have gone. Second, the jobs employing women are nearly all so badly paid that men could not be 'breadwinners' on the wages from them.

Nor is it clear that social harmony would result from a female withdrawal from paid employment. Men may like the idea of being breadwinners, but the evidence on the distribution of those earnings within the household gives no indication that the wages would be devoted to women and children. Married women who take jobs do so to get access to money over which they have some control, a topic addressed in the next chapter.

Before leaving the debate about paid employment, there are two types of work which are strongly gendered: part-time employment and paid work done in the home. Women are much more likely than men to be outworkers or homeworkers: people who perform paid work in their own homes (Phizacklea and Wolkowitz 1995; Crompton 1997). This is the most exploitative type of paid work: the pay is low, the worker provides the premises, heat, light, etc., and receives none of the benefits such as meal-breaks, canteens, access to a pension scheme or holiday pay that regular employees get. The women who do outwork or homework are usually desperate for the money. Women make up the bulk of part-time employees, and while the hours may suit them, they suffer because pro-rata pay is less for part-timers and access to benefits is reduced. The home is a workplace for women, in that women do the bulk of cleaning, cooking and child care, and care for the elderly, sick and disabled. This labour is discussed in the next chapter.

There does appear to have been a major shift in political and public opinion about women's labour market involvement since 1969. The fundamental ambivalence about working women that characterizes British public opinion was revealed in a study by McKay *et al.* (1972). A sample of adults interviewed in Nottingham, consisting of more than 350 people in three areas of the city, were asked about their views on single-parent families and work versus child care. Respondents were asked to say whether a single-parent father should go out to work or stay at home with the children, and then whether a single-parent mother should do the same. Overwhelmingly, the sample chose different work/child care patterns as appropriate for the two genders. Fathers were thought to need paid work for their mental health and self-respect, and often it was felt that a man who stayed home with children was sponging on the welfare state or scrounging. Nor were fathers thought to be good at looking after young children or running homes. In complete contrast, single-parent mothers were considered suitable to rear their children, and it was thought that they should not work full-time. Where any paid employment was considered, part-time jobs were seen as a good idea. Single-parent mothers who could manage to work part-time were thought to benefit from 'meeting people' or 'getting out of the house'; no mentions were made of career-building. Most noticeably, the authors remark: 'No one felt that she should go out to work because it is her place in society or that she should not sponge on the state'.

Carol Smart's (1984) research on divorce included interviews with magistrates in Sheffield. Half the magistrates thought children should live with their mothers after divorce because that was natural, while the rest thought that fathers could not care for children because they had to have paid employment. Sixty-five per cent thought mothers of under-fives should be full-time mothers, and 81 per cent were against the idea that a father should be the home-based parent. Not only should men be in employment, child care by men 'damaged' children.

In the late 1990s, there is no sign that public opinion has changed about single-parent fathers or men in general. Men are expected to be in paid employment, even if they are single parents. Part of the public outcry about 'the problem of men' is the rate of unemployment. On the other hand, there seems to be a change in views about mothers. The Labour government returned in 1997 has a policy of forcing single-parent mothers into the labour market, and there has been little public outcry against the policy.

Verdict

Have women changed as workers while men have not? Certainly there is no evidence that men's attitudes to, or behaviour in, the labour market has changed since 1893 or 1951. There is evidence that women's behaviour has changed since 1951, and that elite women's behaviour has changed since 1893, while the mass of women are working as they did in 1893. The evidence on attitudes to work among women is inconclusive, but the tenor of public opinion has changed. In 1951, it was opposed to mothers working, today it favours it. If there is a change in women's attitudes, it is towards valuing the identity gained from work more, especially among occupations demanding high qualifications. For most women, however, employers still operate a labour market predicated on male values and work patterns, and prejudice, glass ceilings and old boy networks still abound.

Further reading

Crompton, R. (in press) *Women and Employment in Britain*, 2nd edn.

9 Homelife *and* identity: domestic bliss?

> It is the duty of every man, who has sufficient means, to maintain a wife. The life of unmarried women is a wretched one.
>
> (Gissing 1893/1980: 93)

This quote comes from a minor character in *The Odd Women*, Thomas Micklethwaite. He is a maths lecturer at London University, who has been engaged for 23 years while trying to raise enough money to marry. He is just about to achieve his dream and is urging Everard Barfoot to do the same.

The home and the family are seen as the main location for the struggle between women (whose expectations about gender roles and the divisions of emotional, mental and physical labour in the household are believed to have changed) and men (whose expectations about intimacy and domesticity are believed to have remained static). In the light of evidence about emotional work, mental work and physical work in the home, domestic violence, divorce and money management, this chapter explores sex roles in the household and the family. In this chapter, I compare females and males over 25 in their homes and families, contrasting 2001 with the 1890s and with the early 1950s. It is vital to remember that family life can have a dark side: that the home can be a place of misery, violence, abuse and cruelties. We start in Kingsport.

Kingsport University 2006: Scene 9.1

Dolores Jameson, a trainee social worker, is about to start a placement in the refuge for battered women at Maythorpe. She phones her grandmother and mentions her placement in the conversation. Her grandmother says: 'I was talking to my friend Elizabeth about battered women last week: she said there weren't any when *we* were young and blamed television and council estates. But there was a girl at school with us and her mother was always "falling over" and "bumping into doors" – I'm sure *now* her husband hit her, and he was a ticket inspector not a labourer. It isn't new, is it?'

Dolores agrees that domestic violence is not new: 'Refuges are quite new – since the 1970s – but you meet women your age who say that they needed one in the 1930s or 1940s when none existed.

And all sorts of marriages are violent: it's not related to poverty or education. Get her to read Kate Atkinson's novel *Human Croquet*. How's Grampa?'

Dolores's grandmother's friend Elizabeth holds two common beliefs about domestic violence: that it is a modern phenomenon symptomatic of family breakdown and that only uneducated working-class men are violent towards their wives. Neither belief is true.

Domestic violence is one of five aspects of private, domestic life that have been opened up by sociology in the past 30 years. Violence, whether physical or sexual, against spouses, dependent children or the frail elderly, has been studied first to prove its existence and then to try and understand it, with a clear motivation among many investigators to design preventative policies (see Dobash and Dobash 1992). In the same period, other researchers have explored housework (Oakley 1974; Sullivan 1997), money (Pahl 1990; Vogler 1998), caring for dependents (Finch and Groves 1983) and food choice and preparation (Murcott 1983; Charles and Kerr 1988). Researchers have explored marriage, divorce and re-marriage using the insights gained from studies on food, money, violence and housework. When Elizabeth says she does not understand why women remain in violent relationships, she is either revealing that she has not read the literature or she is confessing to a failure of empathy. This chapter begins with a rehearsal of the debates about families, marriage and households in contemporary Britain. It moves from the statistical evidence through the debates about 'changing women and unchanged men'.

It is important to separate the household from the family. Any group of people who sleep *and* eat under the same roof are a household for the purposes of government statistics, although this is not how ordinary people think of it, while those related by blood and marriage are a family. So Wayne Tadman and his fellow soldiers in a barracks, Chloe and her flatmates, and the Crossfields are all households, but only the Crossfields are a family. Most households contain families, but an increasing number of single-person households characterizes contemporary Britain. If we take women's experience of marriage, Britain has seen the average size of household fall steadily all century. In 1901, the average household had 4.8 people in it, today it is 2.4 (*Social Trends* 1999: 42). So there are many more households (there were 16 million households in 1961, 23.6 million in 1998) with fewer people in each. In 1961, 14 per cent of households had only one person in them; in 1998, the figure was 28 per cent (*Social Trends* 1999: 42). Half of single-person households contain an old age pensioner. The proportion of households that are also a traditional family – a couple with dependent children – has fallen steadily since 1961. In 1998, only 23 per cent of households held a traditional family, whereas in 1961 the figure was 38 per cent (*Social Trends* 1999: 42). The lone-parent family household has increased in proportion, but it still only accounts for 7 per cent of all households.

If we take women's experience of marriage, in the 1890s, 1950s and in 2001, and ask what percentage of women ever married, what the average age at first marriage was, and how many children a 'typical' woman had, we do have answers available, because of the government population statistics. It is

Table 9.1 Average age at first marriage

	1931	1951	1961	1971	1981	1991	2001
Women	26	24.6	23.3	22.6		26.3	?
Men	?	26.8	25.6	24.6		28.5	?

Table 9.2 Live births per thousand people

	1951	1961	1971	1981	1991
Live births	72.5	91.6	84.2	62.1	67.00

much harder to find evidence on cohabitation, abortion, domestic violence and money management in households for the 1890s and the 1950s. Data on how women felt about their intimate relationships are almost non-existent and those we have are hard to interpret (on the 1950s, see Finch and Summerfield 1991). Commentators who see the decline of the family and social turmoil in today's patterns are ignoring the realities of family life a century ago, when Gissing wrote *The Odd Women*. Susan McRae (1999) shows that the family of the 1950s and 1960s (sometimes called the 'cereal packet family'), with an intact marriage and 2.4 children, was an unusual 'blip' in long-term trends. In the 1890s and in 2001, both women's age at first marriage and at first childbirth are remarkably similar, as are the proportion of women who never marry and the proportion of childless marriages. 1951 looks different from both 1893 and 2001.

Table 9.1 shows the average age at first marriage from 1931 to 1991. As the average age at first marriage has gone back to what it was in 1931 and in 1893 (allowing novels like those of Bridget Jones to flourish), so too the birth rate has been dropping. Table 9.2 shows the number of live births per thousand people in Great Britain for the census years from 1951 to 1991.

Alternatively, we can consider the total number of live births. In 1901, there were 1.1 million, in 1951 there were 800,000, and in 2001 a total of 700,000 are predicted. Each cohort of women born since 1937 has had fewer children than its predecessor. Or, to put it another way, for every 1000 women aged 15–44 in 1961 there were 91 babies in 1966 and only 59 in 1997. There are two aspects to how many babies a woman has: how many she wants and whether she is able to control her own fertility. The number of children desired has fallen sharply since the 1890s, first in the upper social classes and subsequently in the remainder. One of the 'successes' of the social feminism of the 1918–68 period was to acquire knowledge of, and gain access to, contraception. This spread widely among 'respectable' women, so that they had a better chance of having the number of children *they* felt to be desirable.

In the 1890s, the upper and upper middle classes were more successfully limiting their families than the working classes. By 1951, the whole middle class and skilled manual workers were able to limit their families. By 2001, only a minority of the unskilled working class are still unable to manage contraception. Anne Cartwright (1976) studied people in England and in South Wales in 1967–68 and in 1973. Between these dates, the 'ideal' number of children had declined. In 1973, 18 per cent of married women surveyed wanted either two or three children. Those who already had a boy and a girl felt two was enough; those with two of the same sex preferred three. Cartwright (1976) reported that 20 per cent of married women in 1973 had been 'uncertain' about having children when they married, and 5 per cent did not want children. Thirteen per cent of 1400 women giving birth regretted the pregnancy. Other studies done in this era report similar results (see Delamont 1980: 199–211). As recently as 30 years ago, even married women had difficulty obtaining reliable contraception and managing to use it, and were frequently refused abortions.

These general patterns can lull us into forgetting the class inequalities that underlie them. In 2001, there are clear class differences in the experiences of women around marriage and motherhood. Eighty-seven per cent of women in social classes 1 and 2 are over 25 when they have their first baby; 37 per cent of those in social classes 4 and 5 are under 24. Similar class differences are found among men: those in social classes 1 and 2 become fathers later than those in social classes 4 and 5.

Experience of the end of marriage also has continuities over the period 1890 to 2001, and its consequences for women have remained remarkably similar. In 1890, marriages ended 'prematurely' in death and widows were frequently reduced to poverty. The equivalent today is divorce. In 1890 and 1950, lone parents were predominantly widows and widowers; during the 1960s and 1970s, lone parents were predominantly divorced. In 2001, most lone parents are women who have never been married or divorcees. Widows are, today, rarely parents of dependent children. Divorce, and being a never-married mother, plunge women into poverty. People in social class 1 have the lowest divorce rates, those in the lowest social class, the highest (four times greater). Wives are more likely to petition for divorce today as they were in 1950: this is a change from the 1890s, when the few legal divorces were mostly sought by husbands (McRae 1999). Although there is much media coverage of family breakdown, four-fifths of children live in a family with two parents, nine out of ten of whom live with married parents. There has been a decline since 1972, when 90 per cent of children lived with two parents, but the 'cereal packet' family is still the most common childhood experience (*Social Trends* 1999: 43). British South Asian families are usually larger than others, as are their households, because the extended, three- or four-generation family more frequently shares one home. Single-parent families are most common among African Caribbeans (*Social Trends* 1999: 44).

There is one clear class difference between men and women regarding marriage. By the age of 45, most men and women will have been married at some time in their lives. However, of those who never marry, the men are likely to be unskilled manual workers, while the women are likely to be in social class 1 (Reid 1998). Britain is also characterized by class endogamy; that is, we tend to marry people of the same social class or level of education, or the adjacent social class. Men are more likely than women to marry 'below themselves' in the class hierarchy (Reid 1998).

Family ties may be strong even when the members do not live in the same household. Forty-eight per cent of adults in Britain in 1995 whose mother was still alive saw her *at least* once a week, and 39 per cent saw their father that often. Seventy per cent of people questioned believed that links to close family members should be maintained even if one had little in common with them. Only 13 per cent of informants said they preferred the company of friends rather than family (*Social Trends* 1999: 46).

These facts and figures do not suggest that the British family is in decline or even in crisis. British people seem to value their relatives, and wish to live in marriages or stable cohabitations with children. However, these statistics do not provide any insight into the happiness or misery inside these households or families, or into the physical work or the emotional labour carried out, or the economic arrangements that are made. Divorce has certainly risen in Britain over the past 50 years, partly because the law has changed, but we need high-quality sociological research to discover what everyday life in the family and the households is like, rather than polemical moral panics about the 'end of the family' (Dench 1994, 1996).

The issue of marriage is central to Dench's (1994, 1996) work on men in contemporary Britain. In a pair of polemical books, Dench argues that feminism has gone too far and that men have become detached from society and their financial responsibilities for children. Among the working class, men are too often turning at worst to crime and at best to welfare dependency idleness. His argument is essentially the same as that perpetrated by the conservative feminist Catherine Beecher in the mid-nineteenth century, who argued that America's economic, political and social stability depended on women sacrificing themselves for the greater good. Beecher claimed that women should run happy, healthy, religious homes and sacrifice any other ambitions, feelings or desires so that America could be a stable democracy (Sklar 1973). In 1951, the American functionalist Talcott Parsons produced essentially the same argument (although he did not acknowledge Beecher). Dench is therefore writing in a long, if sexist, tradition.

Dench reached his conclusions in part from an empirical study of 221 people in London that he carried out in 1994–95. He found, like many previous studies, that the beliefs people hold about desirable or ideal sex roles and responsibilities in families and marriage (what ought to happen) are not related to how they actually live themselves. Huber and Spitze (1983) had reported this in the USA, and Dench found the same. Thus people who are divorced may believe that divorce is bad for society, those who are cohabiting may believe in marriage, and mothers in paid employment may believe that full-time motherhood is preferable for children and society.

To evaluate whether the family is in crisis with terrible consequences for men, *and* whether either sex has changed since 1893 or 1951, we can use Dench's data alongside a range of other studies done since the 1950s. Dench argues that there are two different types of family culture in contemporary Britain, one he calls 'traditional' or 'conventional', the other 'alternative'. The latter is similar to what Young and Willmott (1973) called the 'symmetrical family' or Rapoport and Rapoport (1976) termed a 'dual career family'. Dench uses 'alternative' as a negative term: Young and Willmott's label is less value-laden. For Dench, the traditional or conventional family is one where the man is the main breadwinner and the woman the main homemaker, and where all members of the family should provide reciprocal support. This type of family is seen as central to a stable society. Essentially, it is similar to what Bernstein (1971) terms a 'positional family' as well as Young and Willmott's symmetrical family. The 'alternative' family in Dench's model is Bernstein's personal family. Here each person negotiates roles, duties and workload in ways that suit them as individuals and are best for their family, not bound by stereotypes of sex roles, age or position in the family. The best cook cooks, the best driver drives, the person most attached to his or her job works the longest hours and does least at home, and so on. Two-thirds of Dench's interviewees believed in the superiority of the positional family; one-third believed the personal was morally better. A few people lived in a 'traditional' family but believed in a 'personal' one. Dench describes them as 'confused'.

Dench states that older people, those who were or had been married, and parents, were more enthusiastic about the positional family, while the young, the child-free and women in full-time work were keener on the 'personal'. Dench draws from this a doom-laden and conservative message: he claims that the chattering classes are destroying the traditional family even though most ordinary people can see it is essential for social stability. He also argues that the 'personal' family allows men to escape from their moral and financial duties, to the long-term detriment both of the man and society as a whole. This view of men, as selfish, wicked skivers who will abandon their children unless shackled to them, and of women, who must behave like the wives in 1950s sitcoms if Britain is to avoid a crime wave, is deeply depressing. It is grounded in a naive 'biology', which assumes that men are unable to behave in cooperative or egalitarian ways. Dench's conviction that only a traditional, positional family is desirable for both sexes, children and society is over-simplistic. There are issues of class, of labour market experience and of sex differences that need to be explored. Additionally, we need to separate the emotional aspects of family life from the practical and material, and face up to the dark side of the family too. A man who routinely rapes his wife and beats his children with a belt may be very happy with his family life: the victims of his aggression may not be as content.

To explore the wider range of research on the family, I have drawn on the ideas of Bernstein. Dench appears to be unaware of Bernstein's (1971) arguments about the relations between class and family type. Bernstein argued that the upper class and most of the working class lived in 'positional' families (where roles are fixed by age and sex) because this reflected and prepared children for the labour markets they experienced. In the middle classes, Bernstein argued a split had occurred between the old middle class, who worked with property, money and material goods, and the new middle class, who handled symbolic property (psychiatrists, advertising and public relations, the arts, etc.). The old middle class kept to the positional, traditional family; the new middle class had evolved the personal family (see Delamont 1989, 1995). If Bernstein is correct, men with different labour market experiences in different sectors of the middle class will value different types of family. Bernstein's argument, that some sectors of the middle class whose business is the manipulation of symbolic property live in different types of family from the 'old' middle class, is more plausible than Dench's condemnation of the personal family as a feminist mistake, or a mirage espoused by the young, the naive and 'career' women. To summarize, it makes sense to see different family types grounded in the class and labour market experiences of the adults, who will try to rear children to 'fit' the outside world as they have experienced it. As the world of work diversifies, so too does the family. Dench believes that only one type of family 'works' for British society; more sensitive commentators know that different types of family can 'work', and the Dench 'traditional' family can be a hell of violence, inequality and misery.

Apart from his pessimism, Dench is typical of most famous family researchers in Britain. His data are from *London*. Most of the best known research on the family in Britain has been conducted in London, and may not be generalizable to Aberdeen, Belfast, Cardiff or Wigan: far less to tourist towns, rural areas, farms or popular retirement communities such as North Wales or the Isle of Wight. There are classic studies of families in Swansea (Rosser and Harris 1965; Bell 1968) and Banbury (Stacey 1960; Stacey *et al.* 1975) and some more recent ones on naval families in Plymouth (Chandler 1989), farming families in the south west (Wallace *et al.* 1994), the north of England (Christensen *et al.* 1997) and in Wales (Hutson 1990), but none of them have displaced the dominance of London. The most famous research, such as that of Firth (1956), Bott (1957), Gavron (1966), Young and Willmott (1973), Oakley (1974) and Wallman (1984), may never have been generalizable to life elsewhere in Britain. Dench's findings do echo those of Bott (1957) and Young and Willmott (1973), but he fails to address the problems facing women in traditional families found by Gavron (1966) and Oakley (1974).

When Bott (1957) studied marriage in London in the 1950s, there were two discernible styles of marriage. In the first, the man and woman led very separate lives, each spending non-work time with same-sex peers or relatives, so the women sought intimacy with their mothers and sisters. The good husband brought home a wage packet, but was not meant to be a confidante. In the other, the partners were companions, spent leisure time together and sought intimacy with each other. Bott termed the first type 'segregated', the second 'joint'. She looked at the family and neighbourhood relationships of the couples, and found that couples with 'joint' relationships were likely to have 'loose-knit' family and neighbourhood networks, while those with segregated roles had 'close-knit' family and neighbourhood networks. The working-class couples were much more likely to have the close-knit networks and segregated marriages; the middle-class couples were more likely to have loose-knit networks and joint marriages. Finch and Summerfield (1991) set Bott's data in a wider national context.

Twenty years later, Young and Willmott (1973) argued that the English middle classes were moving from an emotionally joint relationship based on a segregated division of labour where the man earned but did no domestic work, and the woman did not earn but did all the domestic work, to a more symmetrical relationship in which the household work and child care were

Table 9.3 Different labels for types of family

Dench	Traditional or conventional	versus	alternative
Young and Willmott	Traditional	versus	symmetrical
Rapoport and Rapoport	Traditional	versus	dual career
Bernstein	Positional	versus	personal
Bott	Segregated	versus	joint

shared, as both man and wife had paid employment. They argued that, as time passed, the same pattern would spread to the working classes as well. In 2001, we can assess how far Young and Willmot were correct. Women have continued to take up paid employment, but there has been very little sign of the symmetry in domestic work, and few signs of the spread of Bott's joint sex roles and companionate intimacy. Rather, the increase in divorce suggests there has been a breakdown in the common understandings of where to seek companionate intimacy. It is *possible* that more women wish to live in joint marriages, while many men do not. The data on the sexual division of labour in the family is presented later in this chapter, after some thought about segregated and joint marriage in modern Britain. Table 9.3 summarizes the terminologies used by the authors mentioned so far.

We are short of data on everyday life in contemporary marriages and inside cohabitations in suburban and urban Britain. The research that has been conducted focused more on the instrumental aspects of life inside households than on the intimacies and emotional temperature. Duncombe and Marsden (1995) conducted interviews with 80 heterosexual couples, and their data are our main sociological source on this aspect of married life. The problem pages of the women's magazines suggest that there are incompatibilities between the sexes in their idea of marriage in 1999. A regular 'problem' comes from a wife who feels that she has not achieved the level of emotional intimacy with her husband that she needs, or deserves, or wants. (Occasionally, a man's letter, in which he is puzzled by his wife's unhappiness, is printed, but women's letters appear much more regularly.) For example, in *Woman* (16 August 1999):

> I've been married for 11 years and have three children. To the outside world we're the perfect family, but I'm not in love with my husband any more. For years he's just done his own thing, going out with his mates every night. I've slowly got used to it, so when he does stay in it puts me off my routine. He spends no time with the family and I often feel like a single parent who happens to be married. He's done nothing to help bring up our kids. The real me is screaming to get out of this trap, but I'm scared to tell him it's over. What if I leave and I'm still not happy? I'm confused.

The agony aunt suggested that the man's behaviour might be explained by him holding the view that he is 'doing enough by supporting his family financially'. That is, she proposes the man believes that intimacy is not part of marriage: he is living one of Bott's segregated marriages. One can argue that this is a letter manipulated for the magazine's readers, but Ann Oakley (1974) described just such a marriage (that of Sally Jordan) 30 years ago in *Housewife*. Mansfield and Collard (1988), reporting a study of 60 newlywed couples, found the women were disappointed that marriage had not produced emotional reciprocity, a close exchange of intimacy, a common life of empathy. The men refused to talk about love and intimacy at all, or reduced the whole agenda to sex. Lewis and O'Brien (1987) found a parallel lack of emotional intimacy with children.

Duncombe and Marsden (1995) report that in their own study women told the interviewer they wanted their partner to signal attachment, by 'unprompted' intimate or romantic gestures and actions, because these would make them feel emotionally 'special'. The men in the study 'appeared' neither to understand nor accept their wives' desires. They either reduced the issue to sex, or felt that they were working so hard to provide economically for their families that they had nothing left to give. Women wanted the emotional intimacy and romantic specialness before sexual intercourse; men wanted the sexual intercourse to serve as the intimacy and romance. Duncombe and Marsden titled their 1995 paper 'Workaholics and whingeing women' to emphasize this gulf between the sexes.

In the context of this research, the letter and the response from the advice columnist seem less like one magazine's attempt to attract readers, and more like an articulation of a research respondent. Nor does it seem to be a problem of younger women. The first writer, married 11 years, is probably in her thirties. In an older generation, the same difficulties can arise. In *Woman's Realm* (10 August 1999), an older woman wrote:

> My husband and I have been married for 29 years and he's never been easy to live with – he's selfish, moody and lazy. I desperately need his support just now but he won't help. He's behaving very strangely, with certain subjects always triggering particular actions. These subjects include holidays, my diabetes, my unemployment, anniversaries, our home and the need to buy anything. When one of these comes up, he starts one of the following: picking a spot until it bleeds, smelling his hands, rubbing his eyebrows, twirling a strand of hair – and then gets really angry. I try to talk about all this but he says it's because I'm complaining. I've seen a counsellor, who said I should consider leaving but I'd rather try to save our marriage. I've told my husband his attitude makes me feel neglected and have asked if he wants me to leave. He always says no but I don't know if that's because he loves me, or doesn't want to do the chores himself.

Here a woman wants an emotional intimacy and, apparently, shared decisions, as did another older woman whose letter was published in *Chat* (18 September 1999):

> My husband's obsessed with his racing pigeons! He does less and less around the house, or for the business we run – he leaves it all to me. We have no conversation, and he's tired all the time. We're only in our early 50s, but never have sex any more. When he called me useless

the other day, I began to wonder whether it's worth hanging on to this marriage.

Chat's agony aunt, Sue, wrote in reply:

> I have a new theory about what's really happening to men and women at the end of this century. I think women are taking over. Not because they want to, but because they have no choice. I know lots of women who are supporting their men, financially and emotionally. They work, look after their kids, organise the finances, do the housework, and still pick up his dirty socks. Not surprisingly, lots of them, like you, often wonder if there's any point to being married at all.

These letters suggest women wanting Bott's joint marriages or Young and Willmott's symmetrical ones, while the men they live with would prefer segregated ones. These three men are ideal husbands in Dench's terms, because they are still there, but it is hard to dismiss these women's views as implanted by feminists or the chattering classes. Perhaps in earlier generations these women would have sought emotional intimacy with female kin. In Harman's (1993) terms, this is the century gap: the women *want* symmetrical families with joint roles, their husbands apparently do not.

One problem with the argument between Harman and Dench is that they are both dealing with an *abstraction*: what an ideal marriage/family would and should be like. Alongside studies of the emotional aspects of marriage, such as that of Duncombe and Marsden, is the research on how the material aspects of marriage are managed. If we turn to the detailed sociological research on 'the private', we can explore what real relationships are actually like.

Unpicking 'marriage': the scrutiny of the private

The research on the 'general' – what sex roles people like to see in marriage – deals with very *abstract* ideas. Much of the sociology of the past 25 years has been about the apparently mundane: Who pays the rent? Who buys the children's school shoes? Who empties the kitchen bin? Who cleans up when granny soils herself? Who hits whom? Whose hobbies get time and money, whose get squeezed out? (see McKie *et al.* 1999). The three plaintive letters are partly about love, shared intimacy and conversation, but they are also about money (the pub, the need to buy anything, pigeons), time ('my routine', holidays, 'tired all the time'), housework, and so on. The research on these phenomena are brought to life by such letters.

Let us start with the research on money. Pahl (1990) pioneered research into the ways money was used inside British households, based on interviews with 100 couples. Her original study found four different ways in which couples organized their money, a typology expanded in her later work. Subsequently, Vogler and Pahl (1994) interviewed 1200 couples in six towns. They distinguished between strategic control and the day-to-day management of money. The poorer households, where money management is an endless struggle, a chore, a burden, more usually have everyday money management in the hands of women. Wealthier households, where money can be used for fun, more frequently have male money management.

Six ways of organizing money management are commonly found in Britain: female whole-wage, male whole-wage, housekeeping allowance, pooling with female management, pooling with male management, and pooling with joint management. (Two per cent of couples keep their money entirely separate, and this is an unexplored 'system'.) The female whole-wage system was a feature of working-class families in areas of heavy industry, such as mining or steel manufacture. A good husband handed his unopened wage packet to his wife, who gave him back 'pocket money' and then ran the household finances. The male whole-wage system keeps all the money in the man's hands. He pays all bills and takes the wife to the shops where he pays for the goods. She has no money, unless she earns some or collects the child benefit. The housekeeping allowance system involves the man giving the woman a fixed amount of 'housekeeping', which she is to use for specified purposes. Women in such households may not know what the man earns, and the 'housekeeping' may not be related in any clear way to the costs of what it is meant to cover. The pooling systems involve all sources of incoming money being brought together (into one bank account, or one teapot) and then dispersed. There can be female, male or joint control over spending from the joint pool.

Pahl had become interested in money management after a study of domestic violence victims who had fled to a refuge. Her informants included women whose husbands earned large wage packets, but spent most of their earnings on drink, gambling or hobbies, leaving the children hungry and ill-clad. She then investigated how non-violent households organized money. In Vogler and Pahl's (1994) study, the more egalitarian systems – the pooling systems – were associated with women in full-time work and better educated men (with 'A' levels or above) with non-traditional views about gender. Men with fewer qualifications and traditional ideas about male and female roles were more likely to follow a housekeeping allowance system. However, the system men grow up with also affects the one they operate; that is, if a man's father used the housekeeping allowance, he is likely to do so too. The housekeeping system is closely associated with an ideology of a male breadwinner. Women who feel they lack control over money are likely to place a high value on earning some 'of their own' when they take paid employment, because they can spend it without feeling they need to ask permission. Vogler (1998) argued that the ways in which money is organized set the agenda for talk about family finance. For example, if the household works on a 'housekeeping allowance' system, discussion will be about the size of that allowance, not about the proportion of the man's wage that he keeps for himself.

The research on money is paralleled by the studies of housework. When Ann Oakley (1974) set out to study housework as work, in 1968 her topic was seen as 'odd'. That research, on forty London housewives with small children, became a pioneering classic. Two findings were strikingly novel in the early 1970s. First, the hours spent. On average, housework took women 77 hours a week, far longer than most jobs. Second, the class difference.

Working-class women liked the role and disliked the tasks; middle-class women hated the label but did not mind the chores. They had far better working conditions (central heating, unlimited hot water on tap, fitted carpets, washing machines, freezers and vacuum cleaners) and got pleasure from interacting with their small children. Working-class women lacked good working conditions and faced conflicts between their child care and the housework. For example, if washing has to be carried down several flights of stairs to the pavement before being done in a laundrette, manipulating a pram, a toddler and the washing is hard work. Reading to a toddler while the washing is in your own machine in your own kitchen is not the same experience. Since Oakley's original study, research has diversified, so that both men and women are studied, as are households early in their life cycle and those of the elderly, families where there are two wage earners or none, with and without children, and so on.

Sullivan (1997) had time diaries from both partners in 408 couples. These data enable us to see not only which sex does which task, but which tasks are done together and which alone. These data come from the SCELI study in six cities in Scotland and England, not just London. Men's domestic work is mainly gardening and DIY, women's is mainly cooking and cleaning. Women frequently report doing more than one task at once: 'washing-up while at the same time operating the washing machine and keeping an eye on the children' (p. 231). It appears that domestic tasks are *still* gendered, and that women are more likely to be doing several at once. Valentine (1999) reports a survey by a major supermarket chain of 43,000 respondents. Women did the bulk of the shopping in 62 per cent and the cooking in 75 per cent. In the households of these respondents, the traditional division of labour was more prevalent in the working-class households than the middle-class ones (or was *reported* as more traditional). Baxter and Western (1998: 101) comment that:

> Most research still shows a clear division of labour within the household with men participating mainly in outdoor work and women taking primary responsibility for childcare and indoor activities such as cooking, cleaning and laundry . . . Moreover wives spend over twice as much time on domestic work as their husbands.

However, women usually tell researchers they are satisfied with the division of labour. Baxter and Western (1998) had data on 2780 men and women in Australia. In their sample, women spent 42.6 hours per week on housework and home maintenance, plus 12.7 hours on child care. The equivalent figures for men were 16.1 and 5.3 hours respectively. Only 13–14 per cent of women report dissatisfaction with the division of labour. Among men, 96 per cent were satisfied with the childcare arrangements and 97 per cent with housework arrangements. Women who believed in the superiority of traditional gender roles were more satisfied with their division of labour than those with a 'feminist' outlook; less educated women more satisfied than the better educated. Perhaps most interestingly, the more men did in the household, the more satisfied the women were, and the nearer the workload was to 50/50, the happier women were.

British studies have produced findings similar to that of Baxter and Western (1998). For example, Mansfield and Collard (1988) found that newly married couples adopted a stereotyped division of labour. The taken-for-granted division of labour can be seen clearly when it is disrupted by divorce, death, incapacity or male homosexuality. Men who have chosen to live without women have to do housework (or pay for it to be done). Coxon (1983) attended an evening class called 'cooking for men'. He found he was the only man in an intact marriage and living with a woman at the class. All the other men were either single (divorced, widowed, orphaned) or gay. There were two distinct subcultures in the same cookery lessons with very different attitudes to food. Both subcultures were 'only' learning to cook because they expected to live in households without women, but for one subgroup this was a necessity (widowers, divorcees, orphans) and for the other a choice (gay men). The straight men wanted to learn to cook plain British basics, like cottage pie or roast lamb, while the gay men wanted to make dishes like quiches and paella. One of the interesting features of the straight men in Coxon's class was that they had only decided to learn to cook when they had exhausted the supply of female relatives. There was a clear pattern of men being fed by mothers, daughters, aunts, sisters, daughters in law, or any female relative. Only when no woman was available did they decide to learn to feed themselves.

There is evidence that women continue to provide domestic care for able-bodied adult children long after they could share the work. Twenty years ago I argued that women continued to perform domestic duties for relatives (such as adult sons) as a hedge against loneliness – as an insurance policy (Delamont 1980: 218–21). None of the research since has changed this analysis. By providing domestic services, women ensure that they are not lonely: the child who comes home with a load of laundry *has come home*. Research on such apparently mundane issues as housework, cooking and money is illuminating about the 'big' topics of power, gender and identity. Women's continuing performance of domestic work for children, men and elderly relatives is a striking continuity in modern Britain. Underneath the talk about families and their changing place in Britain, the work goes on, women feel that shopping, cooking, cleaning, child care, elder care and even family happiness are their responsibility. If women are not shouldering the bulk of the physical and emotional labour they feel *guilt*, so they continue to perform the bulk of the cooking, cleaning, shopping, clothes maintenance and child care. The research on divorce and on new families after divorce (e.g. Burgoyne and Clark 1983) shows how divorcés, and those who establish new families after divorces, have to renegotiate the division of physical and emotional labour, with added burdens of guilt. The same issues of responsibility and guilt predominating in women's lives show well in the research on caring and on domestic violence.

There is a clear relationship between gender and caring. While elderly and disabled married women may get care from husbands (Taraborrelli 1993; Arber and Ginn 1995), most carers are female, who bear the double burden of the physical labour and the guilt. The caring that starts with motherhood extends far into the future, while the duties of being a daughter loom on the horizon (Lewis and Meredith 1998). Dilemmas around caring are another regular feature of the problem pages:

> My sister looks after our elderly father. I couldn't have him myself as I live in a small flat and work full-time. She has a big house, works part-time and is better off than me. Recently, she asked if I'd take Dad so she could have a break. Although I wanted to help, it came at a very bad time, so I suggested a few alternative dates and even offered to pay for Dad to go into respite care, but my sister's taken the huff and won't speak to me. Help!

Woman (9 August 1999) carried this problem, while the following week *Woman's Realm* (17 August 1999) printed:

> My father is now in his seventies and not in the best of health. I also fear that he's depressed, though he puts on a brave front for me. His home used to be spotless – even after Mum died – but it's now a tip and he won't let me clean up. Nor will he let me see his bank statements and I'm worried he may be short of money. Dad was a sergeant in the army for many years and has always been such a strong man – physically and emotionally – that it breaks my heart to see him like this. I can't make him accept my help and I know if I called Social Services he'd never speak to me again. But please, who can help me help him?

Here we see both physical burdens – the sister wanting a break – and emotional ones – the ties to fathers who need care. In both cases, the women writing feel *guilt*. They feel that the care of these men is their problem.

Domestic violence may seem an odd issue to link to caring, but one of the regular findings is that the *victims* of domestic violence feel guilt. They feel that if only they were better cooks, better mothers, better managers, better wives, the men would not hit them. Their self-esteem vanishes and they self-blame.

The dark sides of the family

One of the major achievements of feminist sociology has been the recognition of, and research on, the dark sides of family life (Dobash and Dobash 1992, 1998). The re-discovery of domestic violence in the 1970s (it had been a feminist campaign topic in the 1870s), and the establishment of refuges, was followed by a body of research. Greater recognition of the other five ways in which families may be sites of abuse followed. The six types of abuse are shown in Table 9.4. Such a typology does not include mental cruelty, which frequently accompanies the other types. All six types produce stigmatized victims, who are ashamed to tell 'outsiders' of their injuries.

It is very hard to estimate how many families contain abusers, and the official statistics are notoriously unreliable. Young children and the elderly may be unable to report abuse; many other victims are too frightened to do so, or unaware of where to go or whom to tell. In the early 1970s, the police in the UK were very unwilling to record complaints of domestic violence, so

Table 9.4 Six types of abuse in families

Against	Physical	Sexual
Children	1	2
Women	3	4
The Elderly	5	6

the incidents they discovered did not make it into any statistics. In the summer of 2000, *The Observer* (16 July 2000) claimed that there had been an explosion of domestic violence, but it is more likely that public tolerance, police tolerance and victim tolerance have declined sharply, so that fewer women suffer in private silence. When the girlfriends and the wives of celebrities reveal that they have been beaten up (as a former girlfriend of the retired cricketer Boycott and the ex-wife of soccer player Gascoigne have done), it is possible that the stigma may be starting to decline.

Domestic violence is the best researched of the six dark sides and has led to the biggest efforts towards protecting victims and changing society. Dobash and Dobash (1992) trace the rise of the social movement against domestic violence. They describe the establishment of refuges for victims, the attempts to change the law, to alter the practices of the police, the sentencing decisions of the courts, and to find ways to treat violent men. (These are particularly controversial, with strong claims put forward by practitioners and evaluators that schemes do and do not work.) At the heart of the debates around domestic violence is an issue of power. Men who batter their wives are exercising control over them, because they believe they have a right to do. Women report being beaten up because 'his tea was too weak' (Pahl 1985), 'there was too much grease on his breakfast plate' (Dobash *et al.* 1977), they asked for money to feed the children, they asked where their men had been, he was drunk, he had lost at gambling, they had smiled at the butcher, they were asleep when he came home, because, because, because . . . At the root of the violence is a man's belief that he has a right to control *his* wife, *his* children, *his* household. Studies of male aggressors show that they rarely express guilt; rather, the victims feel guilty.

Police recognition of domestic violence has grown over the past 30 years, together with a reluctant recognition of the physical abuse of children. There is much less acceptance that there can be rape in marriage, that children are sexually abused, or that old people may suffer both physical and sexual abuse. Children are taught to fear 'strangers' not 'Uncle Fred', even though they are more in danger from family and friends than from any stranger.

It would be absurd to argue that there is more domestic violence, rape in marriage, child abuse or elder abuse today than in 1951 or 1893. Rather, researchers, charities and government agencies face up to the problems and force them onto the public agenda. However, it is equally absurd to write about the family, as Dench and Harman do, without recognizing that when it is bad it is very, very bad for those without power.

Verdict

Have women changed either their behaviour in, or their expectations of, marriage since 1893 or 1951, while men have not? Frankly, we cannot know. We know far more about the material sides of marriage and about the dark sides. We do not know whether more people of both sexes want to live in personal families, in symmetrical households, because we do not have the data on 1951 or 1893.

Further reading

Pilcher, J. (1998) *Women of their Time*. Aldershot: Ashgate.

10 Conclusions: *the* verdict

The World is moving.

(Gissing 1893/1980: 336)

If your father goes around saying he likes ballet, or that you like ballet, then he runs the risk of someone else saying – men don't do that. That scares the shit out of him. Same for your mother. . . .
  They don't seem scared. They seem positive.
  That's a clue. Too much positive is either scared or stupid or both. Reality is uncertain. Lots of people need certainty. They spend their lives trying to be what they're supposed to be and being scared they aren't. Quiet desperation.

(Parker 1985: 128)

These two quotes were written 100 years apart. Rhoda Nunn tells a friend that the organization she and Miss Barfoot run is flourishing 'like the green bay-tree' and they are starting a newspaper. The world was indeed moving in 1893. In the Robert Parker quote, his hero, Spenser, is helping an adolescent boy escape from his estranged parents, who have rigid ideas about sex roles, so he can become a ballet dancer. Just as Gissing was asking his readers to widen their ideas about what *women* could do, Parker expects his to expand their horizons about *maleness* and *masculinity*. Strangely, while popular novelists in the nineteenth century like Gissing, and throughout the twentieth century, like Winifred Holtby and Robert Parker (see Delamont 1996), are excited about the opportunities created by what they see as the genderquake, some social scientists are terrified and want to go back. Fukuyama (1999), for example, in *The Great Disruption*, wants women to leave the labour market to men and retreat to the domestic sphere.

While I was writing the book there was a full-blown moral panic about the supposed underachievement of boys in schools, and a steady trickle of articles in the quality papers about 'the problem of men'. For example, David Aaronovitch (*Independent*, 27 May 1999, p. 3), Richard Reeves (*Observer*, 22 August 1999, p. 22), Jack O'Sullivan (*New Statesman*, 28 February 1997, pp. 28–9) and *The Observer's* extracts from Susan Faludi's (1999) *Stiffed* on 4 September 1998. Additionally, there were authors claiming that one or other of two new sciences rendered feminism, gender studies and all social movements and social policy aimed at gender equality redundant. These new 'sciences' are claimed to be either brain-based, in which male and female brains are wired differently, or evolutionary, in which the legacy of our Palaeolithic ancestors is alive in our psychology (see Rose 1998; Rose and Rose 2000). Exactly similar ideas were put forward at the end of the last century. There were moral panics about the feminization of education, about the lack of a role for men, and claims that new work in bioscience 'proved' that feminism had been a terrible mistake which was against 'nature'. The end of a century, especially when there is any advance by feminism, always produces outbreaks of new pseudo-sciences claiming that any change in women's roles is doomed because it is 'against nature'.

In a climate of media 'panic' about failing boys and disaffected men facing yet another wave of pseudo-science 'proving' that I am unfit to be writing this book, debates within feminism seem a distraction. I am still not sure whether postmodernism is so hostile to women's best interests that I should join its opponents, or such a fascinating idea that I should follow Patti Lather (see Delamont 2000b, forthcoming).

What is the verdict on the central question? Have women changed their behaviour and attitudes since 1893 or 1951 while men have not? A cool-headed review of the evidence suggests that British men and women are behaving much like their great-grandparents in 1951 and even their great, great, great, great-grandparents in 1893: most marry, most are close to their families, most work for most of their lives, and so on. Women still do most of the domestic work and the emotional work of households; men in every social class still command the best jobs at that socio-economic level. That is, within social class 2, men are better placed in teaching, social work, libraries and parallel posts in commerce and industry than women. Social class and poverty are more important than gender in the determination of life chances, as they were in 1893 and 1951. Women's opportunities have widened, but class differences between women are more powerful than any gender-based similarities. Men have not changed: but women have not changed either. Adolescent girls have higher aspirations and more credentials, but for most of these young women their credentials are *not* transferred into labour market success or egalitarian marriages. When Beck (1994: 27) argued that 'A society in which men and women were really equal . . . would without doubt be a new modernity', he was describing some far distant future, not Britain in 2001. We can hope that he is describing 2008, but I doubt it.

References

Abbott, P. and Wallace, C. (1990) *An Introduction to Sociology*. London: Routledge.

Abraham, J. (1989a) 'Teacher ideology and sex roles in curriculum texts', *British Journal of Sociology of Education*, 10(1), 33–52.

Abraham, J. (1989b) 'Gender differences and anti-school boys', *The Sociological Review*, 37(1), 65–88.

Abraham, J. (1995) *Divide and School*. London: Falmer Press.

Acheson, D. (1998) *Independent Inquiry into Inequalities in Health*. London: The Stationery Office.

Adkins, L. (1995) *Gendered Work*. Buckingham: Open University Press.

Aggleton, P. (1987) *Rebels Without a Cause*. London: Falmer Press.

Albrow, M. (1996) *The Global Age*. Cambridge: Polity Press.

Allen, I. and Dowling, S.B. (1999) 'Teenage mothers', in S. McRae (ed.) *Changing Britain*. Oxford: Oxford University Press.

Annandale, E. (1998) *The Sociology of Health and Medicine*. Cambridge: Polity Press.

Annandale, E. and Hunt, K. (eds) (2000) *Gender Inequalities and Health*. Buckingham: Open University Press.

Arber, S. and Ginn, J. (eds) (1995) *Connecting Gender and Ageing*. Buckingham: Open University Press.

Arnot, M., David, M. and Weiner, G. (1996) *Educational Reforms and Gender Equality in Schools*. Manchester: Equal Opportunities Commission.

Arnot, M., David, M. and Weiner, G. (1999) *Closing the Gender Gap*. Cambridge: Polity Press.

Askew, S. and Ross, C. (1988) *Boys Don't Cry*. Milton Keynes: Open University Press.

Atkinson, P. and Silverman, D. (1997) 'Kundera's *Immortality*', *Qualitative Inquiry*, 3(3), 304–25.

Back, L. (1996) *New Ethnicities and Urban Culture*. London: UCL Press.

Bailey, L. (1999) 'Refracted selves?', *Sociology*, 33(2), 335–52.

Ball, S. (1980) *Beachside Comprehensive*. Cambridge: Cambridge University Press.

Banks, O. (1981) *Faces of Feminism*. Oxford: Martin Robertson.

Barker, C. (1998) 'Cindy's a slut', *Sociology*, 32(1), 65–82.

Barker, D.L. (1972) 'Keeping close and spoiling', *The Sociological Review*, 20(4), 569–90.

Barrett, M. (1980) *Women's Oppression Today*. London: Verso.

Bates, I. and Riseborough, G. (eds) (1993) *Youth and Inequality*. Buckingham: Open University Press.

Bauman, R. (1982) 'Ethnography of children's folklore', in P. Gilmore and A.A. Glatthorn (eds) *Children In and Out of School*. Washington, DC: Centre for Applied Linguistics.

Baxter, J. and Western, M. (1998) 'Satisfaction with housework', *Sociology*, 32(1), 101–20.

Beck, U. (1992) *Risk Society*. London: Sage.

Beck, U. (1994) 'The reinvention of politics', in U. Beck, A. Giddens and S. Lash (eds) *Reflexive Modernization*. Cambridge: Polity Press.

Beck, U., Giddens, A. and Lash, S. (eds) (1994) *Reflexive Modernization*. Cambridge: Polity Press.

Bell, C. (1968) *Middle Class Families*. London: Routledge & Kegan Paul.

Bennett, A. (1999) 'Rappin' on the Tyne', *The Sociological Review*, 47(1), 1–24.

Bernstein, B. (1971) 'On the classification and framing of educational knowledge', in M.F.D. Young (ed.) *Knowledge and Control*. London: Macmillan.

Best, R. (1983) *We've All Got Scars*. Bloomington, IN: Indiana University Press.

Beynon, J. (1985) *Initial Encounters in the Secondary School*. London: Falmer Press.

Blake, C. (1990) *The Charge of the Parasols*. London: Virago.

Borneman, J. (1992) *Belonging in the Two Berlins*. Cambridge: Cambridge University Press.

Bott, E. (1957) *Family and Social Network*. London: Tavistock.

Bourdieu, P. (1996) *The State Nobility*. Cambridge: Polity Press.

Bowie, F. (1993) 'Wales from within', in S. Macdonald (ed.) *Inside European Identities*. Oxford: Berg.

Bradley, H. (1996) *Fractured Identities*. Cambridge: Polity Press.

Brannen, J. and O'Brien, M. (eds) (1996) *Children in Families*. London: Falmer Press.

Breugel, I. (1996) 'Whose myths are they anyway?', *British Journal of Sociology*, 47(1), 175–7.

Bringa, T. (1995) *Being Muslim the Bosnian Way*. Princeton, NJ: Princeton University Press.

Brodribb, S. (1992) *Nothing Matters*. Melbourne: Spinifex Press.

Brown, P. (1987) *Schooling Ordinary Kids*. London: Methuen.

Brown, P. and Scase, R. (1994) *Higher Education and Corporate Realities*. London: UCL Press.

Burgess, R.G. (1983) *Experiencing Comprehensive Education*. London: Methuen.

Burgoyne, J. and Clark, D. (1983) 'You are what you eat', in A. Murcott (ed.) *The Sociology of Food and Eating*. Aldershot: Gower.

Busfield, J. (1974) 'Ideologies and reproduction', in M. Richards (ed.) *The Integration of a Child into a Social World*. Cambridge: Cambridge University Press.

Butler, I. and Shaw, S. (eds) (1996) *A Case of Neglect?* Aldershot: Gower.

Canaan, J. (1986) 'Why a "slut" is a slut', in H. Varenne (ed.) *Symbolizing America*. Lincoln, NB: University of Nebraska Press.

Canaan, J. (1996) 'One thing leads to another', in M. Mac an Ghaill (ed.) *Understanding Masculinities*. Buckingham: Open University Press.

Caplan, P.J. (1993) *Lifting a Ton of Feathers*. Toronto: University of Toronto Press.

Cartwright, A. (1976) *How Many Children?* London: Routledge & Kegan Paul.

Catchcart, B. (2000) *The Case of Stephen Lawrence*. Harmondsworth: Penguin.

Chandler, J. (1989) 'Marriage and the housing careers of naval wives', *The Sociological Review*, 37(2), 253–76.

Chapman, M. (1978) *The Gaelic Vision in Scottish Culture*. London: Croom Helm.

Chapman, M. (1992a) 'Fieldwork, language and locality in Europe, from the North', in J. de Pina-Cabral and J. Campbell (eds) *Europe Observed*. London: Macmillan.

Chapman, M. (1992b) *The Celts*. New York: St. Martin's Press.

Charles, N. and Kerr, M. (1988) *Women, Food and Families*. Manchester: Manchester University Press.

Christensen, P., Hockey, J. and James, A. (1997) 'You have neither neighbours nor privacy', *The Sociological Review*, 45(4), 621–44.

Clarricoates, C. (1987) 'Child culture at school', in A. Pollard (ed.) *Children and their Primary Schools*. London: Falmer Press.

Coffey, A. and Acker, S. (1992) 'Girlies on the warpath', *Gender and Education*, 3(3), 249–61.

Coffey, A. and Atkinson, P.A. (1996) *Making Sense of Qualitative Data*. Thousand Oaks, CA: Sage.

Coffey, A. and Delamont, S. (2000) *Feminism and the Classroom Teacher*. London: Falmer Press.

Coffey, A., Hall, T. and Williamson, H. (1998) 'Conceptualizing citizenship', *Journal of Education Policy*, 13, 301–315.

Coffield, F., Borrill, C. and Marshall, S. (1986) *Growing Up at the Margins*. Milton Keynes: Open University Press.

Cohen, A.P. (ed.) (1982) *Belonging*. Manchester: Manchester University Press.

Cohen, A.P. (ed.) (1986) *Symbolising Boundaries*. Manchester: Manchester University Press.

Connell, R.W. (1987) *Gender and Power*. Oxford: Polity Press.

Connell, R.W. (1993) *Schools and Social Justice*. Philadelphia, PA: Temple University Press.

Connell, R.W. (1995) *Masculinities*. Oxford: Polity Press.

Connell, R.W., Ashendon, D.J., Kessler, S. and Dowsett, G.W. (1982) *Making the Difference*. Sydney: Allen & Unwin.

Connolly, P. (1998) *Racism, Gender Identities and Young Children*. London: Routledge.

Coward, R. (1999) *Sacred Cows?* London: Harper Collins.

Coxon, A.P.M. (1983) 'A cookery class for men', in A. Murcott (ed.) *A Sociology of Food and Eating*. Aldershot: Gower.

Cremin, L.A. (1979) *Public Education*. New York: Basic Books.

Crompton, R. (1997) *Women and Work in Modern Britain*. Oxford: Oxford University Press.

Crompton, R. (in press) *Women and Work in Modern Britain*, 2nd edn. Oxford: Oxford University Press.

Davidson, J. (1997) *Courtesans and Fishcakes*. London: Fontana.

Deem, R. (1986) *All Work and No Play?* Buckingham: Open University Press.

Deem, R. and Gilroy, S. (1998) 'Physical activity, lifelong learning and empowerment', *Sport, Education and Society*, 3(1), 89–104.

Delamont, S. (1980) *The Sociology of Women: An Introduction*. London: George Allen & Unwin.

Delamont, S. (1989) *Knowledgeable Women*. London: Routledge.

Delamont, S. (1990) *Sex Roles and the School*. London: Routledge.

Delamont, S. (1991) 'The Hit List and other horror stories', *The Sociological Review*, 39(2), 238–59.

Delamont, S. (1992) 'Old fogies and intellectual women', *Women's History Review*, 1(1), 39–61.

Delamont, S. (1994) *Appetites and Identities*. London: Routledge.

Delamont, S. (1996) *A Woman's Place in Education*. Aldershot: Ashgate.

Delamont, S. (1998) 'You need the leotard', *Sport, Education and Society*, 3(1), 5–18.

Delamont, S. (1999) 'Gender and the discourse of derision', *Research Papers in Education*, 20(3), 99–126.

Delamont, S. (2000a) 'The anomalous beasts', *Sociology*, 34(1), 95–112.

Delamont, S. (2000b) 'Confessions of a ragpicker', in H. Hodkinson (ed.) *Feminism and Educational Research Methodologies*. Manchester: Manchester Metropolitan University.

Delamont, S. (in press) *Feminist Sociology: A Critical Review*. London: Sage.

Delamont, S. and Galton, M. (1986) *Inside the Secondary Classroom*. London: Routledge.

Dench, G. (1994) *The Frog, the Prince and the Problem of Men*. London: Neanderthal Books.

Dench, G. (1996) *Transforming Men*. New Brunswick, NJ: Transaction Books.

Dennis, N., Henriques, F. and Slaughter, C. (1956) *Coal is Our Life*. London: Routledge & Kegan Paul.

Dicks, B. (1996) 'Regeneration versus representation in the Rhondda', *Contemporary Wales*, 9, 56–73.

Dicks, B. (2000) *Heritage, Place and Community*. Cardiff: University of Wales Press.

Dobash, R.E., Dobash, R.P., Cavanagh, C. and Wilson, M. (1977) 'Wifebeating', *Victimology*, 2(3), 608–22.

Dobash, R.E. and Dobash, R. (1992) *Women, Violence and Social Change*. London: Routledge.

Dobash, R.E. and Dobash, R. (eds) (1998) *Rethinking Violence against Women*. London: Sage.

Douglas, M. (1966) *Purity and Danger*. London: Routledge.

Downey, G.L. and Lucena, J.C. (1997) 'Engineering selves', in G.L. Downey and J. Dumit (eds) *Cyborgs and Citadels*. Santa Fe, NM: School of American Research Press.

Duncombe, J. and Marsden, D. (1995) 'Workaholics and whingeing women', *The Sociological Review*, 43(1), 150–69.

Dyhouse, C. (1981) *Girls Growing Up in Late Victorian and Edwardian England*. London: Routledge & Kegan Paul.

Epstein, D., Elwood, J., Hey, V. and Maw, J. (eds) (1998) *Failing Boys?* Buckingham: Open University Press.

Faludi, S. (1999) *Stiffed: Scenes from the Betrayal of Modern Man*. London: Chatto & Windus.

Fewell, J. and Patterson, F.M.S. (eds) (1990) *Girls in their Prime*. Edinburgh: Scottish Academic Press.

Fielding, N. (1994) 'Cop canteen culture', in T. Newburn and E.A. Stanko (eds) *Just Boys Doing Business?* London: Routledge.

Finch, J. and Groves, D. (eds) (1983) *A Labour of Love?* London: Routledge & Kegan Paul.

Finch, J. and Summerfield, P. (1991) 'Social reconstruction and the emergence of companionate marriage 1945–59', in D. Clark (ed.) *Marriage, Domestic Life and Social Change*. London: Routledge.

Fine, G.A. (1985) 'Occupational aesthetics', *Urban Life*, 14, 3–31.

Fine, G.A. (1987) *With the Boys*. Chicago, IL: University of Chicago Press.

Fine, G.A. (1996) *Kitchens*. Berkeley, CA: University of California Press.

Fine, M. (1988) 'Sexuality, schooling and adolescent females', *Harvard Educational Review*, 58(1), 29–53.

Firth, R. (ed.) (1956) *Two Studies of Kinship in London*. London: Athlone Press.

Flax, J. (1990) 'Postmodernism and gender relations in feminist theory', in L. Nicholson (ed.) *Feminism/Postmodernism*. London: Routledge.

Flax, J. (1993) 'The end of innocence', in J. Butler and J.W. Scott (eds) *Feminists Theorize the Political*. New York: Routledge.

Fogelman, K. (1976) *Britain's Sixteen Year Olds*. London: The National Children's Bureau.

Foucault, M. (1979) *Discipline and Punish*. New York: Vintage.

Fox-Genovese, E. (1986) 'The claims of a common culture', *Salmagundi*, 72 (Fall), 134–51.

Frank, A.W. (1990) 'Bringing bodies back in', *Theory, Culture and Society*, 7, 131–62.

Frank, A.W. (1991) 'For a sociology of the body', in M. Featherstone, M. Hepworth and B.S. Turner (eds) *The Body*. London: Sage.

Frankenberg, R. (1966) *Communities in Britain*. Harmondsworth: Penguin.

Frazer, E. (1989) 'Feminist talk and talking about feminism', *Oxford Review of Education*, 15(3), 281–90.

Friedman, F. (1996) *The Bosnian Muslims*. Boulder, CO: Westview Press.

Fukuyama, F. (1999) *The Great Disruption*. New York: Profile.

Furlong, A. and Cartmel, F. (1997) *Young People and Social Change*. Buckingham: Open University Press.

Gabe, J. and Thorogood, N. (1986) 'Prescribed drug use and the management of everyday life', *The Sociological Review*, 34(4), 737–72.

Gavron, H. (1966) *The Captive Wife*. Harmondsworth: Penguin.

Gelsthorpe, L. and Morris, A. (eds) (1990) *Feminist Perspectives in Criminology*. Milton Keynes: Open University Press.

Gewirtz, S., Ball, S.J. and Bowe, R. (1995) *Markets, Choice and Equity in Education*. Buckingham: Open University Press.

Giddens, A. (1981) *The Class Structure of the Advanced Societies*. London: Hutchinson.

Gilbert, N. and Mulkay, M. (1984) *Opening Pandora's Box*. Cambridge: Cambridge University Press.

Gill, M. (2000) *Commercial Robbery*. London: Blackstone Press.

Gillespie, T. (2000) 'Virtual violence? Pornography and violence against women on the Internet', in J. Radford, M. Friedberg and L. Harne (eds) *Women, Violence and Strategies for Action*. Buckingham: Open University Press.

Ginn, J., Arber, S., Brannen, J. *et al.* (1996) 'Feminist fallacies: a reply to Hakim on women's employment', *British Journal of Sociology*, 47(1), 167–74.

Gissing, G. (1893/1980) *The Odd Women*. London: Virago.

Goffman, E. (1963) *Stigma*. New York: Doubleday Anchor.

Gould, S.J. (1998) *Questioning the Millenium*. London: Vintage.

Gouldner, A. (1970) *The Coming Crisis of Western Sociology*. Glencoe, IL: The Free Press.

Graham, H. (1993) *Hardship and Health in Women's Lives*. London: Harvester Wheatsheaf.

Hakim, C. (1995) 'Five feminist myths about women's employment', *British Journal of Sociology*, 46(3), 429–55.

Hakim, C. (1996) *Key Issues in Women's Work*. London: Athlone.

Hall, G.S. (1905) *Adolescence*, 2 Vols. New York: Appleton.

Hall, T. (in press) *No Place Like Home*. London: Pluto Press.

Halsey, A.H., Heath, A. and Ridge, A. (1980) *Origins and Destinations*. Oxford: Clarendon Press.

Hammersley, M. (1977) 'The mobilisation of pupil attention', in P. Woods and M. Hammersley (eds) *School Experience*. London: Croom Helm.

Hammersley, M. (1980) 'Classroom ethnography', *Educational Analysis*, 2, 47–74.

Haraway, D. (1989) *Primate Visions: Gender, Race and Nature in the World of Modern Science*. London: Routledge.

Hargreaves, D. (1967) *Social Relations in a Secondary School*. London: Routledge.

Harman, H. (1993) *The Century Gap*. London: Vermilion.

Harris, C.C. (ed.) (1987) *Redundancy and Recession in South Wales*. Oxford: Blackwell.

Hart, R.A. (1979) *Children's Experience of Place*. New York: Irvington.

Harvey, D. (1989) *The Condition of Postmodernity*. Oxford: Blackwell.

Hawkes, G. (1996) *A Sociology of Sex and Sexuality*. Buckingham: Open University Press.

Heath, A. (1981) *Social Mobility*. Glasgow: Fontana.

Heidensohn, F. (1996) *Feminism and Criminology*. Buckingham: Open University Press.

Herbert, C. (1989) *Talking of Silence*. London: Falmer Press.

Heron, L. (ed.) (1990) *Truth, Dare or Promise?* London: Virago.

Hey, V. (1997) *The Company She Keeps*. Buckingham: Open University Press.

Hillman, M., Adams, J. and Whitlegg, J. (1990) *One False Move*. London: PSI.

Hilton, G.L.S. (1991) 'Boys will be boys – won't they': the attitudes of playgroup workers to gender and play experience, *Gender and Education*, 3(3), 311–14.

Hobbs, D. (1988) *Doing the Business*. Oxford: Oxford University Press.

Hoff, J. (1994) 'Gender as a postmodern category of paralysis', *Women's History Review*, 3(2), 149–68.

Hoff, J. (1996) 'A response to my critics', *Women's History Review*, 5(1), 25–30.

Holland, J. and Adkins, L. (eds) (1996) *Sex, Sensibility and the Gendered Body*. London: Macmillan.

Holland, J., Ramazanoglu, C., Scott, S., Sharpe, S. and Thomson, R. (1991) *Pressure, Resistance, Empowerment*. London: Tufnell Press.

Holland, J., Ramazonoglu, C. and Sharpe, S. (1993) *Wimp or Gladiator?* London: Tufnell Press.
Holland, J., Ramazonoglu, C., Sharpe, S. and Thomson, R. (1998) *The Male in the Head*. London: Tufnell Press.
Holtby, W. (1936/1974) *South Riding*. Glasgow: Fontana Collins.
Huber, J. and Spitze, G. (1983) *Sex Stratification*. London: Academic Press.
Hughes, A. and Witz, A. (1997) 'Feminism and the matter of bodies', *Body and Society*, 3(1), 47–59.
Humm, M. (1992) 'Introduction', in M. Humm (ed.) *Feminisms: A Reader*. London: Harvester Wheatsheaf.
Humphrey, M. (1969) 'The enigma of childlessness', *New Society*, 13 March, pp. 399–402.
Hutson, J. (1990) 'Family relationships and farm business in south-west Wales', in C.C. Harris (ed.) *Family, Economy and Community*. Cardiff: University of Wales Press.
Jackson, S. (1982) *Childhood and Sexuality*. Oxford: Blackwell.
Jacobs, S.C. (1997) 'Employment changes over childbirth', *Sociology*, 31(3), 577–90.
James, A. and Prout, A. (eds) (1997) *Constructing and Reconstructing Childhood*. London: Falmer Press.
Jeffery, P. (1976) *Migrants and Refugees*. Cambridge: Cambridge University Press.
Jenks, C. (1996) *Childhood*. London: Routledge.
Karakasidou, A.N. (1997) *Field of Wheat, Hills of Blood*. Chicago, IL: University of Chicago Press.
Kent, S.K. (1996) 'Mistrials and diatribulations', *Women's History Review*, 5(1), 9–18.
King, A. (1997) 'The Lads', *Sociology*, 31(2), 329–46.
Lacey, C. (1970) *Hightown Grammar*. Manchester: Manchester University Press.
Lambart, A. (1976) 'The Sisterhood', in M. Hammersley and P. Woods (eds) *The Process of Schooling*. London: Routledge & Kegan Paul.
Lambart, A. (1982) 'Expulsion in context', in R. Frankenberg (ed.) *Custom and Conflict in British Society*. Manchester: Manchester University Press.
Lash, S. and Urry, J. (1994) *Economies of Signs and Space*. London: Sage.
Lather, P. (1991) *Getting Smart*. London: Routledge.
Leach, E.R. (1970) *Levi-Strauss*. London: Fontana.
Lees, S. (1986) *Losing Out*. London: Hutchinson.
Leonard, D. (1980) *Sex and Generation*. London: Tavistock.
Lewis, C. and O'Brien, R. (eds) (1987) *Fatherhood Reassessed*. London: Sage.
Lewis, J. and Meredith, B. (1998) *Daughters Who Care*. London: Routledge.
Llewellyn, M. (1980) 'Studying girls at school', in R. Deem (ed.) *Schooling for Women's Work*. London: Routledge.
Lloyd, B. and Duveen, G. (1992) *Gender Identities and Education*. London: Harvester Wheatsheaf.
Lury, C. (1997) *Consumer Culture*. Cambridge: Polity Press.
Lyon, D. (1999) *Postmodernity*, 2nd edn. Buckingham: Open University Press.
McClancy, J. (ed.) (1996) *Sport, Identity and Ethnicity*. Oxford: Berg.
Mac an Ghaill, M. (1988) *Young, Gifted and Black*. Milton Keynes: Open University Press.
Mac an Ghaill, M. (1994) *The Making of Men*. Buckingham: Open University Press.
Mac an Ghaill, M. (1999) *Contemporary Racism and Ethnicities*. Buckingham: Open University Press.
Macintyre, S. (1977) *Single and Pregnant*. London: Croom Helm.
Macintyre, S. (1993) 'Gender differences in the perceptions of common cold symptoms', *Social Science and Medicine*, 36(1), 14–20.
Mackenzie, D. (1999) 'Slaying the Kraken', *Social Studies of Science*, 29(1), 7–59.

Mackridge, P. and Yannakakis, E. (eds) (1997) *Ourselves and Others*. Oxford: Berg.

Mahony, P. (1985) *Schools for the Boys*. London: Hutchinson.

Malcolm, N. (1994) *Bosnia: A Short History*. London: Macmillan.

Mansfield, P. and Collard, J. (1988) *The Beginning of the Rest of Your Life?* London: Macmillan.

Marqusee, M. (1994) *Anyone but England*. London: Weidenfeld & Nicolson.

Marshall, G., Swift, A. and Roberts, S. (1997) *Against the Odds*. Oxford: Clarendon Press.

Mason, D. (2000) *Race and Ethnicity in Modern Britain*, 2nd edn. Oxford: Oxford University Press.

McCrone, D. (1992) *Understanding Scotland*. London: Routledge.

McCrone, D., Morris, D. and Kiely, R. (1995) *Scotland – the Brand*. Edinburgh: Edinburgh University Press.

McCrone, D., Stewart, R., Kiely, R. and Bechhofer, F. (1998) 'Who are we?', *The Sociological Review*, 46(4), 629–52.

McDonald, M. (1989) *We are Not French: Language, Culture and Identity in Brittany*. London: Routledge.

McKay, A., Wilding, P. and George, V. (1972) 'Stereotypes of male and female roles', *The Sociological Review*, 20(1), 79–92.

McKie, L., Bowlby, S. and Gregory, S. (eds) (1999) *Gender, Power and the Household*. London: Macmillan.

McRae, S. (ed.) (1999) *Changing Britain*. Oxford: Oxford University Press.

Meadows, P. (1999) *The Flexible Labour Market*. London: National Association of Pension Funds.

Measor, L. (1984) 'Gender and the sciences', in M. Hammersley and P. Woods (eds) *Life in School*. Milton Keynes: Open University Press.

Measor, L. (1989) 'Are you coming to see some dirty films today?', in L. Holly (ed.) *Girls and Sexuality*. Milton Keynes: Open University Press.

Measor, L. and Sikes, P. (1992) *Gender and Schools*. London: Cassell.

Measor, L. and Woods, P. (1984) *Changing Schools*. Milton Keynes: Open University Press.

Menter, I., Muschamp, Y., Nicholls, P., Ozga, J. and Pollard, A. (1997) *Work and Identity in the Primary School*. Buckingham: Open University Press.

Meyenn, R.J. (1980) 'School girls' peer groups', in P. Woods (ed.) *Pupil Strategies*. London: Croom Helm.

Moberly Bell, E. (1953) *Storming the Citadel*. London: Constable.

Monaghan, L. (1999) 'Creating the perfect body', *Body and Society*, 5(2–3), 267–90.

Morgan, K. and Mungham, G. (2000) *Redesigning Democracy*. Bridgend: Seren.

Murcott, A. (ed.) (1983) *A Sociology of Food and Eating*. Aldershot: Gower.

Murcott, A. (ed.) (1998) *The Nation's Diet*. London: Longman.

Nairn, T. (1977) *The Break Up of Britain*. London: Verso.

Nayak, A. (1999) 'Pale Warriors', in A. Brah, M.J. Hickman and M. Mac an Ghaill (eds) *Thinking Identities*. London: Macmillan.

Newburn, T. and Stanko, E.A. (eds) (1994) *Just Boys Doing Business?* London: Routledge.

Newson, J. and Newson, E. (1965) *Patterns of Infant Care*. Harmondsworth: Penguin.

Newson, J. and Newson, E. (1970) *Four Years Old in an Urban Community*. Harmondsworth: Penguin.

Nilan, P. (1991) 'Exclusion, inclusion and moral ordering in two girls' friendship groups', *Gender and Education*, 3(2), 163–82.

Oakley, A. (1974) *The Sociology of Housework*. Oxford: Martin Robertson.

Oakley, A. (1979) *Becoming a Mother*. London: Martin Robertson.

Oakley, A. (1998) 'Science, gender and women's liberation: an argument against postmodernism', *Women's Studies International Forum*, 31(2), 133–46.

Oakley, A. (2000) *Experiments in Knowing: Gender and Method in the Social Sciences*. Cambridge: Polity Press.

Okely, J. (1983) *The Traveller-Gypsies*. Cambridge: Cambridge University Press.

Osmond, J. (1994) *A Parliament for Wales?* Cardiff: Gomer.

Owens, D.J. (1982) 'The desire to father', in L. McKee and M. O'Brien (eds) *The Father Figure*. London: Tavistock.

Paechter, C. (1998) *Educating the Other*. Buckingham: Open University Press.

Pahl, J. (ed.) (1985) *Private Violence and Public Policy*. London: Routledge.

Pahl, J. (1990) *Money and Marriage*. London: Macmillan.

Pahl, R. (1996) *After Success: Fin de siècle Anxiety and Identity*. Oxford: Polity Press.

Parker, R. (1985) *Early Autumn*. Harmondsworth: Penguin.

Pearson, G. (1983) *Hooligan*. London: Macmillan.

Phizacklea, A. and Wolkowitz, C. (1995) *Homeworking Women*. London: Sage.

Phoenix, A., Woollet, A. and Lloyd, E. (eds) (1991) *Motherhood*. London: Sage.

Pilcher, J. (1998) *Women of their Time*. Aldershot: Ashgate.

Pilcher, J. (1999) *Women in Contemporary Britain*. London: Routledge.

Pilcher, J. and Wagg, S. (eds) (1996) *Thatcher's Children*. London: Falmer Press.

Prendergast, S. (1989) 'Girls' experience of menstruation in schools', in L. Holly (ed.) *Girls and Sexuality*. Milton Keynes: Open University Press.

Procter, I. and Padfield, M. (1999) 'Work orientations and women's work', *Gender, Work and Organization*, 6(3), 152–62.

Pugsley, L. (1998) 'Throwing your brains at it', *International Journal of Sociology of Education*, 8(1), 71–90.

Pugsley, L., Coffey, A. and Delamont, S. (1996) 'Daps, dykes and five-mile hikes', *Sport, Education and Society*, 1(2), 133–46.

Purvis, J. (1989) *Hard Lessons*. Cambridge: Polity Press.

Radford, J., Friedberg, M. and Harne, L. (eds) (2000) *Women, Violence and Strategies for Action*. Buckingham: Open University Press.

Ramazanoglu, C. (1996) 'Unravelling postmodern paralysis', *Women's History Review*, 5(1), 19–24.

Rapoport, R. and Rapoport, R. (1976) *Dual Career Families*. Harmondsworth: Penguin.

Rapport, N. (1993) *Diverse World-Views in an English Village*. Edinburgh: Edinburgh University Press.

Rapport, N. (2000) 'The best of British?', *Anthropology Today*, 16(2), 20–2.

Redhead, S. (ed.) (1993) *The Passion and the Fashion*. Aldershot: Avebury.

Rees, G. and Fielder, S. (1992) 'The services economy, sub-contracting and new employment relations', *Work, Employment and Society*, 6(2), 347–68.

Rees, G., Williamson, H. and Istance, D. (1996) 'Status zero', *Research Papers in Education*, 11(2), 219–35.

Rees, T.L. (1992) *Women and the Labour Market*. London: Routledge.

Rees, T.L. (1998) *Mainstreaming Equality in the European Union*. London: Routledge.

Rees, T.L. (1999) *Women and Work*. Cardiff: University of Wales Press.

Reid, I. (1998) *Class in Britain*. Cambridge: Polity Press.

Renold, E. (1999) 'Presumed innocence: an ethnographic exploration into the construction of sexual and gender identities in the primary school'. Unpublished doctoral dissertation, University of Wales, Cardiff.

Renold, E. (2000) 'Coming out': gender, (hetero) sexuality and the primary school, *Gender and Education*, 12(2), 309–26.

Richardson, D. and May, H. (1999) 'Deserving victims?', *The Sociological Review*, 47(2), 308–31.

Ridley, M. (1993) *The Red Queen: Sex and the Evolution of Human Nature*. Harmondsworth: Penguin.

Riseborough, G. (1993a) 'Learning a living or living a learning?', in I. Bates and G. Riseborough (eds) *Youth and Inequality*. Buckingham: Open University Press.

Riseborough, G. (1993b) 'GBH – the Gobbo Barmy Army', in I. Bates and G. Riseborough (eds) *Youth and Inequality*. Buckingham: Open University Press.

Roberts, H. (1985) *The Patient Patients*. London: Pandora.

Roberts, K. (1993) *Youth and Employment in Modern Britain*. Oxford: Oxford University Press.

Roman, L. (1992) 'The political significance of other ways of narrating ethnography', in M.D. Le Compte, W.L. Millroy and J. Preissle (eds) *The Handbook of Qualitative Research in Education*. San Diego, CA: Academic Press.

Rose, H. and Rose, S. (eds) (2000) *Alas, Poor Darwin*. London: Jonathan Cape.

Rose, S. (1998) *Lifelines*. Harmondsworth: Penguin.

Roseneil, L. (1995) 'The coming of age of feminist sociology', *British Journal of Sociology*, 46(2), 191–205.

Rosser, C. and Harris, C. (1965) *The Family and Social Change*. London: Routledge.

Salisbury, J. (1996) *Educational Reforms and Gender Equality in Schools: Findings from Wales*. Manchester: Equal Opportunities Commission.

Salisbury, J. and Riddell, S. (eds) (2000) *Gender, Policy and Educational Change*. London: Routledge.

Scott, S. and Morgan, D. (eds) (1993) *Body Matters*. London: Falmer Press.

Scott, S., Jackson, S. and Backett-Milburn, K. (1998) 'Swings and roundabouts', *Sociology*, 32(4), 689–706.

Serbin, L. (1978) 'Teachers, peers and play preferences', in B. Sprung (ed.) *Perspectives on Non-Sexist Early Childhood Education*. New York: Teachers College Press.

Sewell, T. (1998) *Black Masculinities and Schooling*. Stoke-on-Trent: Trentham Books.

Sewell, T. (1999) 'Loose canons?', in D. Epstein, J. Elwood, V. Hey and J. Maw (eds) *Failing Boys?* Buckingham: Open University Press.

Showalter, E. (1996) *Sexual Anarchy*. London: Picador.

Smithers, A. and Zientek, P. (1991) *Gender, Primary Schools and the National Curriculum*. Manchester: School of Education, Manchester University.

Sikes, P.J. (1991) 'Nature took its course?', *Gender and Education*, 3(2), 145–62.

Skeggs, B. (1997) *Formations of Class and Gender*. London: Sage.

Sklar, K.K. (1973) *Catherine Beecher*. New Haven, CT: Yale University Press.

Smart, C. (1984) *The Ties that Bind*. London: Routledge.

Smith, L.S. (1978) 'Sexist assumptions and female delinquency', in C. Smart and B. Smart (eds) *Women, Sexuality and Social Control*. London: Routledge.

Social Trends 19 (1989) London: HMSO.

Social Trends 29 (1999) London: HMSO.

Solomon, J. (1991) 'School laboratory life', in B.E. Woolnough (ed.) *Practical Science*. Buckingham: Open University Press.

Stacey, M. (1960) *Tradition and Change*. London: Oxford University Press.

Stacey, M. (1975) *Power, Persistence and Change*. London: Routledge & Kegan Paul.

Stanley, L. and Wise, S. (1983) *Breaking Out: Feminist Consciousness and Feminist Research*. London: Routledge & Kegan Paul.

Sullivan, O. (1997) 'Time waits for no (wo)man', *Sociology*, 31(2), 221–40.

Surridge, P. and McCrone, D. (1999) 'The 1997 Scottish Referendum vote', in B. Taylor and K. Thomson (eds) *Scotland and Wales: Nations Again?* Cardiff: University of Wales Press.

Taraborrelli, P. (1993) 'Becoming a carer', in N. Gilbert (ed.) *Researching Social Life*. London: Sage.

Thompson, A., Day, G. and Adamson, D. (1999) 'Bringing the "Local" back in: the production of Welsh identities', in A. Brah, M.J. Hickman and M. Mac an Ghaill (eds) *Thinking Identities*. London: Macmillan.

Thorne, B. (1993) *Gender Play*. Buckingham: Open University Press.

Titus, J.J. (2000) 'Engaging student resistance to feminism', *Gender and Education*, 12(1), 21–38.

Tobias, S.A. (1990) *They're Not Dumb, They're Different*. Tucson, AZ: Research Corporation.

Trosset, C. (1993) *Welshness Performed*. Tucson, AZ: University of Arizona Press.

Turner, E., Riddell, S. and Brown, S. (1995) *Gender Equality in Scottish Schools*. Glasgow: Equal Opportunities Commission.

Tyler, M. and Abbott, P. (1998) 'Chocs away', *Sociology*, 32(3), 433–50.

Valentine, G. (1999) 'Eating in', *The Sociological Review*, 47(3), 491–524.

Vicinus, M. (1985) *Independent Women*. London: Virago.

Vogler, C. (1998) 'Money in the household', *The Sociological Review*, 46(4), 687–713.

Vogler, C. and Pahl, J. (1994) 'Money, power and inequality within marriage', *The Sociological Review*, 42(2), 263–88.

Walby, S. (1997) *Gender Transformations*. London: Routledge.

Walford, G. and Miller, H. (1991) *City Technology College*. Buckingham: Open University Press.

Walklate, S. (1995) *Women and Crime*. Buckingham: Open University Press.

Wallace, C. (1987) *For Richer, for Poorer*. London: Tavistock.

Wallace, C., Dunkerley, D., Cheal, B. and Warren, M. (1994) 'Young people and the division of labour in farming families', *The Sociological Review*, 42(3), 501–30.

Wallman, S. (1984) *Eight London Households*. London: Tavistock.

Walters, M. (1980) 'Introduction to *The Odd Woman*', in G. Gissing, *The Odd Woman*. London: Virago.

Walum, L.R. (1977) *The Dynamics of Sex and Gender*. New York: Rand McNally.

Warde, A., Martens, L. and Olsen, W. (1999) 'Consumption and the problem of variety', *Sociology*, 33(1), 105–28.

Weiner, G. (1994) *Feminisms in Education*. Buckingham: Open University Press.

Weis, L. (1989) *Working Class without Work*. London: Routledge.

Werbner, P. (1996) 'Our blood is green', in J. MacClancy (ed.) *Sport, Identity and Ethnicity*. Oxford: Berg.

West, J. (1999) '(Not) talking about sex', *The Sociological Review*, 47(3), 525–47.

Willis, P. (1977) *Learning to Labour*. Farnborough: Gower.

Wilson, D. (1978) 'Sexual codes and conduct', in C. Smart and B. Smart (eds) *Women, Sexuality and Social Control*. London: Routledge & Kegan Paul.

Wilson, E. (1980) *Halfway to Paradise*. London: Tavistock.

Wilson, E. (1991) *The Sphinx in the City*. London: Virago.

Wincup, E. (1997) 'Waiting for trial'. Unpublished doctoral dissertation, University of Wales, Cardiff.

Wolf, M. (1992) *The Thrice Told Tale*. Berkeley, CA: University of California Press.

Wolpe, A.M. (1974) 'The official ideology of education for girls', in M. Flude and J. Ahier (eds) *Educability, Schools and Ideology*. London: Croom Helm.

Wolpe, A.M. (1988) *Within School Walls*. London: Routledge.

Woods, P. and Hammersley, M. (eds) (1993) *Gender and Ethnicity in Schools*. London: Routledge.

Woolard, K.A. (1989) *Double Talk*. Stanford, CA: Stanford University Press.

Wyn Jones, R. and Trystan, D. (1999) 'The 1977 Welsh referendum vote', in B. Taylor and K. Thomson (eds) *Scotland and Wales: Nations Again?* Cardiff: University of Wales Press.

Young, M. and Willmott, P. (1973) *The Symmetrical Family*. Harmondsworth: Penguin.

Index

CHANGING WOMEN, UNCHANGED MEN?

Sociological perspectives *on* gender *in a* post-industrial society

Sara Delamont

Open University Press
Buckingham · Philadelphia

Open University Press
Celtic Court
22 Ballmoor
Buckingham
MK18 1XW

email: enquiries@openup.co.uk
world wide web: www.openup.co.uk

and
325 Chestnut Street
Philadelphia, PA 19106, USA

First Published 2001

A catalogue record of this book is available from the British Library

ISBN   0 335 20037 0 (pb)   0 335 20038 9 (hb)

Library of Congress Cataloging-in-Publication Data
Delamont, Sara, 1947–
    Changing women, unchanged men?: sociological perspectives on gender in a
post-industrial society / Sara Delamont.
        p. cm. – (Sociology and social change)
    Includes bibliographical references and index.
    ISBN 0-335-20038-9 – ISBN 0-335-20037-0 (pbk.)
    1. Sex role–History–20th century. 2. Women–History–20th century. 3.
Women–Social conditions. 4. Feminism. 5. Social change. I. Title. II. Series.

HQ1075 .D453 2001
305.3′09′04–dc21   2001021075

Typeset in 9/11pt Stone Serif by Graphicraft Limited, Hong Kong
Printed in Great Britain by Biddles Limited, Guildford and King's Lynn